The Story of Wynberg-Allen School

Excelsior

The Story of Wynberg-Allen School

Rakhshanda Jalil

NIYOGI BOOKS

This book is a collaborative effort between the
WYNBERG HOMES SOCIETY and NIYOGI BOOKS

The Wynberg Homes Society
Bala Hissar, Mussoorie - 248179

Published by
NIYOGI BOOKS
D-78, Okhla Industrial Area, Phase-I
New Delhi-110 020, India
Tel: 91-11-26816301, 49327000
Fax: 91-11-26810483, 26813830
email: niyogibooks@gmail.com
www.niyogibooksindia.com

Text: Rakhshanda Jalil
Photographs: Arvind Hoon, Pankaj Sharma and
Wynberg-Allen School Archives

Sketches: Fatimah Zaidi
Design: Write Media

ISBN: 978-93-83098-11-8
Year of Publication: 2014

Printed at: Niyogi Offset Pvt. Ltd., New Delhi, India

CONTENTS

COURTESY: AJAY MARK

C.B./ Mussoorie 24th Jan. 1890.

Sister R. B. West
New Place
Mussoorie

My dear Sister

At a Meeting today of Bro. Barlow & Patton - Sisters Barlow & Patton & my wife it was resolved (1) that we thankfully accept your offer to be the Head Mistress of the C.B. School &c (2) that as the School expands Miss Rhinds offer be accepted, if you think it advisable, and on our having one talk more about her regarding her maintenance - (3) That Bro West's offer to keep the Cashbook and Ledger be also accepted. In your case & his we will gladly meet board & lodging charges - in yours we will gladly either meet a bill or pay a fair monthly charge for clothing - In all respects we wish sisterly & brotherly confidence and understanding - Kindly come and spend tomorrow with us and bring the

[left margin:] the draft of advertisement & Prospectus and C.M. Gazette with you. Please bring Bro West with you. Yours truly A. Foy Chairman C.B.

[right margin:] The board of your little ones will be met by us. - A. Foy Chairman

The earliest document on file: Letter from the Chairman, Mr Arthur Foy, to Mrs West. 1890.

WYNBERG ALLEN SCHOOL
1888
SCHOOL

Foreword

EXCELSIOR! To strive for excellence, to continue to reach higher levels of performance and achievement despite challenges — with the help and in the glory of the Lord.

In 2013 Wynberg-Allen celebrates a remarkable milestone — a hundred and twenty-five years of continued growth and success. Few institutions in India can claim as rich and treasured a history, one that has brought glory to our nation. Members of the alumni have fought in the great wars of the twentieth century and several have sacrificed their lives in the line of duty. We salute them, one and all.

Today, Wynberg-Allen has the best infrastructure in India spread across two sprawling campuses. Built on a strong foundation of sacrifice, generosity and tireless effort, it provides excellent learning and education without prejudice. Continuing a tradition of effective leadership, dedicated staff and committed students, the School continues to ensure outstanding results in academics, extra-curricular activities and sports, year after year. The School focusses on discipline and overall character development that is based on solid values of hard work, compassion, respect and integrity and where diversity is a rewarding experience.

This book is a well-accounted chronicle. It takes us on a journey that begins with faith and with the planting of a seed one hundred and twenty-five years ago. There were tempests along the way but the seed grew firm; roots turned into saplings and continued to flourish — strong and resolute. Through hurdles and challenges the young tree learned to adapt and though its mettle was often tested it overcame years of struggle and strife. By the turn of the twenty-first century this seed had become a mighty Himalayan oak and today it stands tall among the renowned educational institutions of India.

This tribute honours the visionary founders of the School and pays homage to every member who served Wynberg-Allen diligently, with commitment and sacrifice, since its inception.

Karan Singha, IPS

Chairman, Board of Management, Wynberg-Allen School and Wynberg Homes Society

1888-1908

Of
Faith and Constancy
The Early Years

Take this child away and nurse him for me.

Exodus 2:9

HOW SMALL IS THE SEED! And what faith has to be shown in its sowing! Yet such is God's working that the tiny seed first throws up tender shoots, then digs roots deep into the soil and produces branches and leaves, till the tree can be seen in all its glory, standing tall and strong and firm.

A hundred and twenty-five years ago a seed was sown in good faith. Watered by constant devotion, watched over by caring benefactors, warmed by the light of belief, the tree has borne flower and fruit, provided shade and safe haven, nurtured many a waif and fledgling. Having had the opportunity to go through old documents, principals' reports, logbooks of minutes, minutely detailed accounts of meetings, notes and memos, boxes of photographs and scraps of paper — all immaculately preserved — I am able to see how small was that seed and how great was the faith of those who planted it.

The tree is today known as the Wynberg-Allen School; its story — from its earliest days — as it unfurls in these pages is as much the story of the courage and conviction of a handful of people as it is of the evolution and growth of the School. Also, as we shall see, from a purely philanthropic initiative meant to provide quality education in a healthy environment at highly subsidised fees to a professionally-run, high-ranking school, among the best of the hill schools in Upper India, the Wynberg-Allen School has had a long and eventful journey.

This chapter will record the first milestone of that journey. However, this opening chapter, which is also in the nature of an introduction to this book, will perforce be longer than the others as it will set out many of the goals and objectives that in later years would become the hallmark of the School.

So we laboured at the work...

Nehemiah 4:21

It was some time in the year 1887 that four friends met in Kanpur (or Cawnpore as it was then called); they were: Mr and Mrs Arthur Foy, landed proprietor from Khari, Oudh; Mr Alfred Powell, landowner in Mussoorie; and Dr (Brigade Surgeon) J. H. Condon. The subject closest to their heart was the education of orphaned and destitute children of European and Eurasian descent. While there were several reputed schools for privileged European children already in existence in different parts of the country — several in the salubrious climate of the hills of Upper India, most notably Bishop Cotton School set up in 1859 at Shimla — there were none that concerned themselves exclusively with those with moderate means let alone the poor, the needy and the deprived. And this was a cause of grave concern. Something had to be done.

By the late nineteenth century there existed in India a substantial number of people of mixed descent who were known as Eurasians or Anglo-Indians. And this community, like any other, had its fair share of orphan and destitute children. Then, there were the others: those who, while seemingly a part of the European or Eurasian community by dint of looks or skin colour, were

Left: The seed is sown: Mr and Mrs Foy, Mr Alfred Powell and Dr Condon meet at Kanpur (then Cawnpore) to discuss how to bring their dream to fruition.
Top: Mr Arthur Foy.
Above: Mrs Foy.

Top: Dr J. H. Condon.
Above: Mr Alfred Powell.

nevertheless considered beyond the pale. The offspring of this coupling of the East and West — the twain that Rudyard Kipling had famously declared were destined never to meet — posed a real problem. These children — often called 'orphans' for want of a better word — could neither be wished away nor discarded. Nor could the community shrug away all responsibility towards them. Strenuous efforts of missionaries, such as Bishop Cotton, had brought the Government's attention to the plight of the European and Anglo-Indian children who were growing up in ignorance and destitution and could:

> ...either be a scandal to the English government or a source of strength and influence to the British-named Government in India, depending on whether they are left in their present state of ignorance and degeneration or given an intellectual and practical education to fit them to be useful members of society.[1]

The Government, for its part, too was not unaware of the gravity of the situation. Lord Canning had drawn the Government's attention to the embarrassing possibility of a large, floating population of Indianised English exhibiting the 'worst qualities of both races'. If left unattended, such children would, he warned, 'become a class dangerous to the State and a glaring reproach to the Government and the faith which it will profess, but if cared for betimes will become a source of strength to the British rule and of usefulness in India.'

Despite the gravity of the situation, the Government had showed no inclination to take up the cause of Anglo-Indian education; it was therefore left to the various Christian denominations to raise funds through subscriptions as well as donations. The Government would provide moral and part-financial assistance; the bulk of the expense had to be raised through voluntary enterprise. It soon

[1] C. Lawrence, *Report on the Existing Schools For Europeans and Eurasians*, Calcutta, 1873, p. 3.

became evident that any effort in this direction required the support and goodwill of the larger domiciled European community, those who for reasons of Empire or faith, lived and worked in India, those who understood the frailties of the less-privileged, and were willing to give generously of their time and money to such a cause. Equally important was the need to bring these infants and children into the fold, as it were, to bring them to God. An enterprise of this nature, the four friends meeting at Cawnpore decided, would require the kindly and benign assistance of women as well as men of the cloth. Being Anglicans, it was also decided that the school provide education and training to Protestant children though no needy Christian child would be turned away.

Also, the four friends agreed that the proposed venture must be in the nature of a boarding school-cum-orphanage-cum-training institution and draw needy pupils from all over Oudh and the North-Western Provinces. The name 'Christian Training School and Orphanage', therefore, seemed an appropriate one for an institution that would serve several purposes: provide a safe and healthy home for infants who had been abandoned or were living in indigent circumstances as well

1

Christian Training School & Orphanage.

Meeting of the Committee Christian Training School and Orphanage held at Wynberg on the 2d of June, 1894 at 5.30 p.m.
Present Dr J. H. Condon, Rev. T. Evans, Messrs A. Foy, Alfred Powell, W. W. Johnstone, J. O. N. James & Mrs West.
The proceedings opened with prayer for Divine guidance and blessing by Bro. A. Foy, Chairman.
The Chairman presented the bill submitted by Mr Christie for work done at Wynberg amounting to Rs 1489-9-6 After careful scrutiny the Committee find that some of the charges are higher than prevailing rates, and in addition commission has been charged at 10%. The Committee passed the bill, deducting the 10% commission amounting to Rs 135-6-3 leaving Rs 1354-3-3, and after deducting the advance of Rs 400/- leaving a balance of Rs 954-3-3 to be paid. The Commission is not a legitimate charge when work is done on contract.
The Chairman, Building Fund is authorised to pay the balance of Mr Christie's bill, viz:- Rs 954-3-3.
Mrs. West submitted a memo of necessary urgent repairs; &c. which was made over to Mr. James for his attention.
Mrs West asked for instructions regarding the leave to be given to teachers & matrons during the winter vacation.
The

Minutes of a meeting, 1894.

129

V. Read Sub Committee's report of 8th Oct./98 on the age limit for the admission of Boys & Girls into the C. J. S. & O in future – as follows;–

After long discussion it was resolved that Boys shall not be admitted after the age of Eleven years, nor shall they be allowed to remain in the School after the age of 15 years.

All applications for the admission of boys beyond the age of 11 years must be referred to the Board of Management for approval and Sanction – The continuation of boys in the School after the have attained the age of 15 years must also be sanctioned by the Board.–

Girls shall be admitted up to the age of twelve (12) years – after they have passed this age none shall be admitted without the Sanction of the Board.– Their continuation in the School after the age of Eighteen (18) years will depend on the approval of the Board.–

Every effort should be made to provide for, or secure, suitable employment for Girls who have attained the age of Seventeen years.–

Sd/. J. O. N. James, Alfred Powell, A. H. Jahaund, J. H. Condon –

Resolved that the Sub Committee's report be approved and adopted.–

Question raised by Mrs Hunt – Whether the two Marshalls, Frank Foy & Harry Davies are to be allowed to return to School next year.–

Resolved that Frank Foy be allowed to remain until a place can be found for him.–

Resolved that no other boys above 15 years be readmitted without the special sanction of the Board.–

VI. The Chairman at the conclusion of the meeting tendered his resignation as he was about to leave the country.–

The Board record their special thanks to the Revd. J. M. [illegible] Chairman, for the able assistance he has always so cheerfully rendered to this Institution and at the Boards meetings.–

The meeting

Minutes of a meeting held at Wynberg in 1894. Among those present were Dr J. H. Condon, Rev Evans, Mr Arthur Foy, Mr Alfred Powell and Mrs West.

Butchers &c) be paid for all supplies for the School not later than the 16th of the following month.—
Meeting closed with prayer by Revd Evans.

X X X

A. H. Addis.
Chairman

Minutes of a Meeting of the Board of Management C. T. School & Orphanage, held at Wynberg on Saturday the 26th August 1899 at 12-30 p.m.—

Present. Dr. J. A. London; Colonel Geo: Strahan R.E.; Revd J. Evans. Messrs A. B. Addis C.E.; A. Powell; W. W. Johnstone; H. A. Jahans, J. O. N. James; Mrs Collins; Mrs A. Powell; Mrs Hunt & Mrs James.—

The Revd P. R. Mackay, Secretary Anglo-Indian Evangelisation Society, was present by invitation.—

The proceedings opened with prayer for the Divine blessing and guidance by Coll Geo: Strahan.—

I.— The Revd P. R. Mackay was asked to address the Committee on the proposals he had to make in reference to affiliating this Institution to the Society which he represents.—

Mr Mackay represented to the Board that he felt deeply interested in the welfare of this Institution & after careful & prayerful deliberation had come to the conclusion that it had a great future before it, and considering the wants of India & the necessity of giving boys a good & sound Christian education & of training them to the requirements of the present day, he felt that we would gain great benefit from affiliation with the Anglo Indian Evangelisation Society. The great want at present of this Institution was a Christian & trained tutor for the boys department, such a man as might be obtained through his Society from the Scottish National College of tutors.—

II. Mr Mackay's address was much appreciated by

as basic education for young children followed by some sort of vocational training to older ones to equip them for a life of gainful employment. The area of Mussoorie — given its bracing climate and increasing importance as a colonial outpost — seemed like a good place to start a new school which would focus on health and hygiene as much as sports and a sound Christian education. Without further ado, Mrs Eugenia Catherine West was enlisted. She was the wife of Mr Barton-West who worked at the Himalaya Seed Store in Barlowgunj. Mrs West agreed to come on board as Superintendent, an office she held till her untimely death in 1895.

I will lift up mine eyes unto the hills...

Psalm 121

Bordered by the misty-blue Siwalik Range and the beautiful Doon Valley to the South and the majestic slopes and ridges of the Upper Himalayas to the north, Mussoorie was ideally located. Accessible by rail from Saharanpur and located a bare 14 miles from Dehra Mussoorie (known as 'Mansuri' by the locals after a native shrub, the *Cororiana nepalensis* or the 'mansur'), lies approximately 6,500 feet above sea level. Captain Young, Commandant of the Sirmur Battalion stationed at Dehra, is credited with 'discovering' Mussoorie in 1823. The history of Mussoorie, in colonial records, begins with the establishment of a hunting lodge built by Captain Young and Hon'ble F. J. Shore, the Assistant Collector of Dehra, at a ridge called Camel's Back. The abundance of game in the densely-wooded hills attracted military personnel from Dehra and the surrounding cantonments; soon, the healthy climate began to draw ailing British soldiers, thus considerably increasing traffic to this picturesque hill station. By 1826, the first English dwelling had come up in Landour, the twin town which derived its name from Llanddowror, a village in southwest Wales, in a custom that was reminiscent of the many nostalgic English, Scottish, Welsh or Irish names common during the Raj. This house, which still stands and is pointed out by locals with some pride, was called 'Mullingar' meaning 'the left hand mill' after a town in Westmeath County, Ireland, and was used as an office and residence by Captain Young.

A year later a sanatorium came up a short distance away followed, in quick succession, by shops, boarding houses, banks and post offices; soon, a steady stream of visitors — both sick and healthy — began to take the bridle path from Rajpur near Dehra during the lively 'season'. To meet their needs — both of this world and the hereafter — various institutions came into being: The Old Brewery in 1830, the Landour Cemetery at about the same time, Christ Church in 1836 — said to be the oldest church in the Himalayas. In 1832, Sir George Everest, the Surveyor General of India from 1830-1843, built a house on the 600-acre Park Estate at Hathipaon. Houses began to spring up all along what is now Kulri; some that were built on Pari Tibba (also known as 'Burnt Hill') were exposed to lightning and so construction moved towards Cloud End. The first bank, North East Bank, came up in 1836 and the first club of its kind, the Himalaya Club in 1841; the next logical requirement was a civic body, the Mussoorie Municipal Board, which came up in 1842, and Mussoorie's own newspaper, *The Hills*, started by the indefatigable entrepreneur John Mackinnon. In the same year, Mussoorie received a most unusual visitor, the Amir of Afghanistan, Dost Mohammad, who was sent into political exile soon after the First Afghan War. He was housed at Bala Hissar, named after the fort he had left behind in Kabul; but more on Bala Hissar later since it looms large in the history of the Wynberg-Allen School.

In 1838, an intrepid English woman crossed the Siwaliks in a *jampan* to spend an entire season at Landour. This adventurous woman was Fanny Parks, author of the delightfully engaging travelogue, *Wanderings of a Pilgrim*. Mussoorie and Landour continued to grow all through the 1830s and 40s with many beautiful houses and estates mushrooming on the flats. Major Swetenham is credited with introducing slate roofs and soon the most picturesque bungalows and cottages could be seen among copses of laurels, oaks and rhododendrons. Shops, hotels, restaurants, boarding houses came up to meet the 'seasonal' demands. But by the 1840s a new sort of visitor began to come to these hills in droves — parents in search of good schools — and the hills suddenly came alive with the sound of young voices.

The first of the Mussoorie schools, the Mussoorie Seminary, was begun by John MacKinnon in 1840; it was followed by a few small preparatory schools but the next Big One was the Waverley Convent, established in 1845 by the Religious Sisters of Jesus and Mary Mussoorie Educational Society. This was followed by St George's College in 1853. Set up by the Archdiocese of Patna in a building called Manor House, the school was taken over by the Irish Brothers of the Order of St Patrick in 1894. Next came the Woodstock

School, established in 1854 by a group of Englishwomen called the Society for Promotion of Female Education, followed by the Caineville School in 1864 under an Anglican management.[2] In 1866, a military orphanage, St Fidelis, was moved from Shimla and housed near St George's.[3] As the number of schools in these hills began to swell, the Biddulph Summer Home was established in 1870 for children of British military officers, but this was a 'seasonal' affair meant to cater to families who came up to the hills to escape the sweltering heat of the plains. As word of Mussoorie's invigorating weather and fresh spring waters as well as easy accessibility by road began to spread, yet another school opened in 1888: Oak Grove meant exclusively for the families of those who worked in the Eastern and the North-Western railways. Of all the Mussoorie schools, this had the largest number of Anglo-Indian pupils since the maximum number of positions, at various levels in the railways, was occupied by the Anglo-Indians.

[2] After 1947, with dwindling Anglican pupils, the remaining students were transferred to the All Saints School in Nainital and the Caineville School was shut down.
[3] St Fidelis too was shut after 1947; in this case because most of its pupils were from what is now Pakistan.

A year ago, in 1887, the Christian Training School and Orphanage — that would later transform into the Wynberg Homes and eventually the Wynberg-Allen School — had already come into being. Unlike the other schools that existed in Mussoorie till then, its impulse was primarily philanthropic. Save for St Fidelis, none catered to the poor and downtrodden, none strove to combine an educational mission with a Christian one in quite the same manner. What is more, none grew from such modest beginnings.

Jaberkhet, where Wynberg-Allen started in 1890 as the Christian Training School and Orphanage.

Behold I show you a mystery: We shall all be changed:
From glory to glory.
Corinthians 15:51

The Christian Training School and Orphanage began life in a rambling old house on a heavily-wooded hilltop called Jaberkhet, along a bridle path from Landour to the old township of Tehri.

Pack mules used to bring food, and provisions up the steep incline to the School.

Situated on a clearing, it afforded commanding views of the valley below but, given its position on a promontory, was also susceptible to thunder and lightning as well as the worst of the Monsoon rains. What is more, being so isolated, its grounds were frequented by leopards and other animals of the wild. With neither running water nor electricity, the good Mrs West and her charges were dependent on water brought up from a mountain stream by the bucket full, kerosene lamps for light and wood fires for warmth. Food, provisions, and just about everything else had to be fetched up the steep incline by pack mules. Dr Condon, one of the early benefactors of the School, rode up to keep a watchful eye on medical eventualities.

The building, now considerably tumbledown and decrepit, is known locally as the Haunted House. Few know it by its proper name; fewer still know it as the birthplace of the Wynberg School. Occasionally visited by picnickers and by truant school boys and girls till a few years ago, visitors are now kept at bay by a vigilant security guard hired by the present owner. The property, having changed hands over the years, is called Rockville and is practically uninhabitable. A motorable road has

lessened its isolation but one can well imagine how lonely it must have been a hundred and twenty-five years ago.

Under the circumstances, Mrs West was evidently a woman of great courage and resolve. The School started with precisely two students, both orphans: Peter and Mary Cables; of the two, Mary later joined the school as an apprentice teacher. The numbers increased to six pupils and then 12 till a fire caused extensive damage to the building and forced the school to look for new premises. Mrs West moved, briefly, with her charges to two houses, Abbotsford and Dunedin in the Castle Hill Estate, which now houses the office of the Survey of India. But by 1896 the School's patrons were able to secure premises in a location that continues to be part of its present campus, namely the estate called Wynberg Hotel near what was then called the Mussoorie Hotel.

By the fifth year of its existence, that is, by 1893, the School was being run in a fairly organised manner. By now, it had a Managing Committee comprising: Brigade Surgeon J. H. Condon, Reverend W. J. P. Morrison, Reverend T. Evans, Reverend Dennis Osborne, Messrs. W. W. Johnstone, Alfred Powell and C. T. Robbie. Its Chairman and Treasurer was Arthur Foy; Mrs Foy, along with Mrs Collins, Mrs Hurst, and Mrs Powell served on the House Committee and little Miss Foy, who had studied at Woodstock School, pitched in as an honorary music teacher. Mrs West, in her Superintendent's Report for the year 1893, writes:

> This School was originated some four years ago through the agency of Mr and Mrs Foy and a few other kind friends who felt the urgent need of a thorough Christian Institution, which would afford sound English education in a good climate, to the children of parents whose means would be too limited, to allow them to secure such a privilege for their children in any other hill school. We are happy to be able to say that though the School began in a very small way, it has gone on, through the blessing of God, increasing in its numbers

> and usefulness since its commencement to the present time, and there are now over 60 children enjoying the privileges of this Benevolent Institution.

While the School was 'thoroughly unsectarian' in principle, two-thirds of the pupils were wards of Church of England parents. Mrs West describes the criteria for admission thus:

> Our principle for admission is, to take in as many as our funds will allow, of the most *needy*, and our only regret is, that we are not able to provide funds and accommodation for many more such worthy objects of help, while we have many urgent applications which we have reluctantly to refuse.
>
> The rule for fees is ten per cent of the salary of the parent for *each child*, so that in case the father's pay is only Rs. 50, the child is received for Rs. 5 per month, and we have now

Mrs West taking care of her charges at the Orphanage at Jaberkhet.

> in the school some twenty-three children whose parents can only pay from Rs. 5 to Rs. 10 per child, while others pay from Rs. 10 to Rs. 15 and there are twelve children for whom nothing is paid. We have one child whose parents can pay Rs. 20 and one Rs. 25.

This being the case, two facts are self-evident:

> I. That this school supplies a long-felt want for the education of poor children in a hill climate. There is no other like it, in the whole of the N.W.P...
>
> II. ...that the above rate of fees scarcely meets one half of the current expenses of the school, the balance is contributed by kind Christian friends ...The cost of each child to the school, including all expenses, comes up to Rs. 15 a month, the total of which amounts at present to about Rs. 900, while all the fees realised from the children amount to about Rs. 400.

Training in the Scripture, readings from the Bible as well as moral instructions went hand in hand with the teaching of lay subjects. The Examiner's Report, prepared by C. H. DeMello, Retired Inspector of Schools for N.W.P., gives a detailed account of subjects taught, the number of children in each class as well as their ages, which in 1893 ranged from infants to 12 years located as they were in the Infants Home or in Standards I to V.

Thanks to the kindness of friends, gifts in cash and kind began to pour in, as a result of which the School managed to remain free of debt. Those who knew the good work being done here told their friends who, in turn, told others. The School also published a magazine called *Christian Citizen* in which it listed its achievements and informed the public about its activities. For a short while, a four-page leaflet called *Indian Witness* was also published for distribution among friends of the School.

Mrs West with her flock of destitute children.

Teachers, including Mrs West, took only a nominal amount as board and lodging; several Mussoorie ladies volunteered to give music lessons free of charge to those pupils whose parents could not afford the additional fee of Rs. 6 per month for piano lessons. Since the largest expenditure was on rent for the two hired premises (after the house at Jaberkhet burned down), it was resolved to buy a suitable property at the earliest — one that would be large enough to accommodate more children, as well as have a playground and additional classrooms and dormitories. With about Rs. 1,600 paid a year as rent annually, and the landlord threatening to increase it to Rs. 2,000, the School decided to raise funds somehow and to buy a house that had recently come up for sale. A Committee was formed and J. H. Condon, Thomas Evans and Arthur Foy made a passionate appeal to the domiciled Christian community to rise to the occasion: to help the Christian Training School and Orphanage 'secure the suitable building which is now available'.

H. G. Meakin, of Poona, responded to the appeal and donated the princely sum of Rs. 20,000. Not one to rest on its laurels, the School Committee appealed for contributions towards the cost of supporting the extra children that could now be accommodated, as well as constructing suitable premises for the staff to be housed close to the children. Cash amounts — ranging from Rs. 1,000 sent by T. T. Bond of Cawnpore to Rs. 500 sent by an anonymous 'Lover of the Cause' to Rs. 5 and Rs. 3 by individuals scattered across the length and breadth of Imperial India — poured in for the Building Fund; donations and subscriptions towards fees, clothes, medicines, special treats, etc. added up to a grand total of Rs. 11,135 for the year 1893. Monies were collected from nearby Landour, Dehra, Saharanpore, Unnao, Agra, Meerut, Cawnpore as well as far-away Calcutta, Bombay, Abbotabad, even a sum of Rs. 48 from an M.P. (a certain S. Smith) came all the way from London. Various schemes were floated by earnest and well-meaning individuals: musical concerts in Dehra and Saharanpore as well as house-to-house calls in the bigger stations to collect no more than a rupee a month from *every* domiciled family, in short, all manner of 'schemes' were devised in the sincere belief that money given to the needy is money 'lent to the Lord', and He pays the best interest.

Inasmuch as ye did it to one of the least of these, ye did it unto me.
Jesus Christ

All along, the School functioned on one basic principle: The Lord Shall Provide. Those at the helm of the School's affairs firmly believed that as soon as the need arose, the Lord would, in some unexpected way, have it met. A new dormitory for boys, lavatory and bathrooms, a larger classroom, a room set aside as a sick room — somehow the kindness of benefactors ensured that these expenses were met. Making a passionate appeal on behalf of her young charges, Mrs West writes:

> To those who are familiar with the life of the poor Europeans in Indian towns, there can be no sadder sight than the numbers of neglected children growing up in ignorance and vice. To rescue

School children with Mrs West, 1903.

Fresh air and exercise for both boys and girls.

such children is not only the privilege, but the urgent duty of every Christian man or woman who can help, either with time or money, and as we are doing a little of this, we would earnestly entreat them to render such help, as would enable us to widen the field of our labours.

No sooner had Meakin donated a handsome amount to the school, he also presented the School with its new home: the Wynberg Hotel Estate, a beautifully located property with the Raspanna Nadi on the east, bound on the west by the road going to Landour, on the north by the Oaks Estate, and the Seven Oaks Estate, Constantia and Cedar Hall on the south with the bridle path to

Rajpur running through it. What is more, Meakin instructed the architect, J. O. N. James: 'Debit the cost of the Dormitory and improvements to me.' Meakin had bought the Wynberg property for the School in memory of his son who had died tragically at the age of six; Meakin himself died before he could execute the deed of gift but his widow and two remaining children honoured his wishes and the Wynberg Estate was transferred to the Trustees of the Christian School and Orphanage on 9 December 1896. Though, it was several years before the School came to be known by its present name, and the property continued to be referred to by locals not as Wynberg but as 'Bobbi sahib ka Hotel', apparently by the name of the last owner, a certain Bobby Heseltine. As to the name 'Wynberg' (meaning 'wine mountain' in Afrikaans), one has not been able to ascertain its origins. There is a suburb of the city

Preparing a meal during a Domestic Science class.

of Cape Town in South Africa called Wynberg and another close by called Constantia; the former developed from a small farming community to a British garrison town in 1804. Its major attractions include vineyards and the Wynberg Boys' High School set up in 1841. A connection, if any, with the School at Mussoorie has not been established, nor is it known if the previous owners — or the neighbours at Constantia — had a South Africa connection.

During the long, hard winter months, several children who either had nowhere to go or lacked the money for travel, stayed back. Mrs West reports 23 children (of the 60 on roll) who stayed back in 1894; the school ensured they stayed healthy and active despite the cold that can be severe in the Upper Himalayas. Once again, the good people of Mussoorie rallied around to ensure they had a good time during the festive season. A practice was started — of collecting money for gifts — that continued for decades with the management setting aside some money for 'treats'. Also, the tradition of Fancy Fair was started, a tradition that the School maintains till this day. A group of ladies who had involved themselves in the running of the School, helped out in different ways: in conducting examinations, taking classes in cookery, drawing, sewing, singing or scripture reading as well as collecting items for sale to raise funds during Fancy Fair. These ladies included Mrs Foy, Mrs Condon, Mrs Powell, Mrs Johnstone, Mrs James, Mrs Johnson, Mrs Hooper, Mrs Kinlock, Mrs Griffith, Mrs Collins, Mrs Christie — all familiar names since their husbands too, in most cases, either served on the Board or helped the School in several discreet ways. Rev Hooper of the All Saints Church is still remembered with a Hall named after him.

From the earliest days, the Union Church played an important role in the School and its working. For one, the Pastor and his wife helped in every way they could with Rev Evans not merely serving on the Board as Chairman after Arthur Foy's health declined in 1898, but also taking weekly lessons in 'Bunyan's

Pilgrim's Progress' and the children attending Sunday service followed by Sabbath School. Mrs Evans helped gather clothes — both new and used but in good condition. She also encouraged the good ladies of Mussoorie to stitch flannel vests, shirts, pinafores, etc. for the children thus easing the burden on parents. A Christian Endeavour Class was started with different members taking turns to conduct the classes once a week — either at the

The Wynberg Orphanage, circa 1907.

School or at the Church — depending on the weather being fair or inclement.

On 24 February 1894, the School moved to the location that would become its lasting abode — Wynberg. By now, it had 84 boarders and 9 day scholars, of which 34 were boys. Two houses adjoining Wynberg were bought — Cedar Hall and Constantia — for a sum of Rs. 12,500; of which Rs. 11,000 was borrowed from the Alliance Bank and Rs. 1,500 paid from the fund collected for the Infants' Home. Of these two new houses, the former was used for classrooms and as Principal's quarters and the latter as an infants' home. Unfortunately, shortly thereafter, Mrs West, who had displayed exemplary courage and fortitude in managing the School's affairs so far, began to show symptoms of debilitating rheumatism. Already, she had forsaken her salary in lieu of the board and tuition of her four children. As the rheumatism gradually spread to her hands, Mrs West had to perforce lay down her pen and her second daughter, Miss Ethel West, increasingly began to help with the School's duties such as writing the Annual Report for the year 1895.

The School got its first Principal in B. Dukoff Gordon who began the practice of taking the children out on long walks and rambles in the surrounding mountainside and encouraged outdoor games and sports. The girls were taught calisthenics three or four times a week and the boys had drill as well as games of cricket and football. Mr Gordon, in his first report as Principal for the year 1896, notes:

> We are anxious to have a good school rather than a large one — a well organised and well taught school rather than one only numerically strong — a school from which youths and maidens shall go out well equipped by both character and intellectual training for the serious business of life. We wish this to be a school full of healthy, elevating, hallowing influences; above all a school conducted on sound Christian principles...

While the School continued to grow and increase its holdings as well as take in more children, the demand for admissions too grew apace, especially from poor parents or widows who needed a safe haven for the children's education and upkeep. Education in all subjects, including Urdu, was given strictly in accordance with the Code of Regulations for European Schools (since the School became eligible to accept Grant-in-Aid) and the first batch of students for the Government Primary Examination were presented in 1895.

Unfortunately, almost immediately thereafter, the faith of this small community was put to the test and the smooth functioning of the School was marred by two events: the sudden death of H. G. Meakin, the School's chief benefactor at Carlsbad, the Austrian watering hole, on 1 June 1895; and the tragic passing away of Mrs West in December 1895. Mrs West, who suffered from rheumatism, had over the past year been supervising the running of the School from her sick-bed and relying upon her daughter, Ethel. Upon Dr Condon's advice she left for a warmer climate in late October 1895 but reached no further than Saharanpur where she died of rheumatic pericarditis.

Mrs West's grave in the Mussoorie Cemetery on Camel's Back Road.

Suffer little children to come unto me.
Jesus Christ

Elections for free scholars were held annually on the basis of nominations or recommendations by a well-known authority or a friend of the School. The Managing Committee scrutinised every application most carefully and the logbook of the minutes, kept in the School's archives, notes details of discussions into the merits of each and every case. The School faced its first serious financial crunch in 1897 when subscriptions and donations were reduced to a trickle due to circumstances beyond anyone's control. The Great Famine of 1896-97, with its epicentre in Bundelkhand, had devastated large parts of the United Provinces and killed over one million people. Prominent newspapers had launched

a Famine Fund and several philanthropic institutions in India and England were busy collecting aid for the famine stricken. With hunger stalking the countryside, there was precious little left over for institutions such as the Christian Training School and Orphanage at Mussoorie. The Government's Grant-in-Aid of Rs. 2,901 helped tide over this difficult time, as did the tidy sum of Rs. 1,287 raised through concerts and Fancy Fair.

Incidentally, in accepting the Grant-in-Aid offered by the Provincial Government's Department of Education, from 1896 onwards, the School was increasingly obliged to follow rules and regulations regarding employment of teachers as well as the conduct of examinations, syllabi for teaching, and inspection from the Board of European Schools. The Great Despatch of 1854 had already laid down the foundations of modern education in India and introduced a system of grants-in-aid to help support the rising number of privately-managed educational institutions. Since the Government's policy of religious neutrality excluded the missionary schools from financial aid, schools such as the one at Wynberg benefitted; its prospectus proclaimed its status as 'non-denominational' and while pastors and reverends served on its Board (in later years as Principals too), and the School followed Anglican principles, it remained, in theory, 'non-conformist' and 'thoroughly unsectarian'.

Lord Lytton's famous Minute on 'The Education of the Children of Poor Europeans and Eurasians' (1880) had stressed the need for vocational training or avenues of employment after leaving school, such as jobs in railways, telegraphs, armed forces or specific government departments for this neglected section of the country's population. Mindful of this, the School at Wynberg still retained 'Training School' in its name and proposed the starting of a training school for teachers on its premises. The Inspector of Schools' reports had suggested improvements in the quality of teachers, and this the Board of Management readily agreed to do by hiring experienced educationists for the senior classes instead of earnest folk who agreed to take on teaching positions for a nominal board and lodging but with a primary impulse to 'do good'. The Inspector also suggested that the 'poorer girls' who would be passing out after Standard VII, be given 'further training such as practical lessons in domestic economy, needle work, and any subject likely to be of use in domestic service. The girls who were in better circumstances who wished to become teachers... to be taught more advanced general lessons, and to be instructed on (sic) methods of teaching.' Orphan or destitute girls with nowhere to go were allowed to stay on at the School, and occasionally paid

Professionally conducted nurses training in preparation for a secure future.

a pocket money of Rs. 3 to Rs. 5 and expected to 'generally make themselves useful'.

As one century limped towards its end and a new one was waiting to be born, the Christian Training School and Orphanage at Mussoorie found itself on the cusp of change. It had achieved much, but a great deal more was waiting to be done. In the fifteen years of its existence it had carved a niche for itself:

- From precisely two students on its rolls under the charge of a lone lady superintendent, it now had 5 teachers and 100 students;
- From a ramshackle house on a deserted hilltop, it now owned considerable properties in a far more accessible — and genteel — part of town; and
- From an informal classroom with children of varying ages to pupils distributed age-wise in Standards ranging from I to VII.

A sad blow was dealt to the small community at Wynberg with the death of Arthur Foy on 25 February 1901. Foster father of this home of the poor and one of the chief architects of the movement to start an orphanage-cum-training school in the hills, he served as the first Chairman and remained till the end a true friend, an indefatigable fund-raiser and supporter of the School. Dr Condon, another founder-patron, had to leave Mussoorie on account of his health. But for each loss, there was a commensurate gain. New friends joined the circle. A new internationalism wafted through the School premises with Mr J. H. MacGoun, an Australian, joining the School as Principal, and Miss Grace Browne, a trained teacher from America, taking charge as Head Mistress.

In 1901, too, the first batch of girls passed out. Once again, friends of the School found suitable 'situations' for them. While most went into service, some took hospital training while others found openings as assistant teachers in mission schools. In accordance with the rules laid down for Government-aided schools, the Christian Training School and Orphanage at Wynberg began to give increasing importance to what was deemed 'industrial' work. Besides the two hours a week spent on mending their own clothes, they were also taught 'plain and fancy' sewing work and dressmaking as well as plain and advanced cookery. The older girls were put in charge of the wardrobe of younger ones and also taught to lay the table and attend at meals as well as given duties in the dormitories, library, dining hall and school rooms. Classes in typing and shorthand were started in 1903 and printing and woodwork for boys a year later.

As word spread of the good work being done at the School, items for sale at the annual Fancy Fair began to come from far and wide. Donations of food items, pharmaceutical products and assorted household items were gladly accepted and readily sold to fetch a tidy sum for the School each year. The Statement of Accounts for 1903 shows the average cost of feeding a child as being Rs. 7-1-9. The Grant-in-Aid sufficed to meet teachers' salaries and the amount raised from Fancy Fair and Concerts went towards the salaries of servants and house staff. A mysterious 'Lover of the Cause' bore the cost of winter food for those who stayed back. The balance of the expenditure, that is, on clothes, lighting, repairs, occasional purchases, etc. was met by donations. Donation boxes were put up in Churches to collect funds for the School. The School closed the year 1903 with a debit balance of Rs. 1,899-8-1, a debit lingering since its purchase of Cedar Wood and Constantia. On the credit side, it had an ever-increasing circle of friends — kind, considerate, caring friends who helped out with gifts in cash and kind: a new cooking range, curtains, framed pictures, beds, benches, desks and chairs, a new knitting machine, book cases, the laying of a new cemented floor in the classrooms, Christmas treats for those who had nowhere to go, uniforms, books and clothes for those who couldn't afford new ones. Those who could not help in cash helped in kind: flour at reduced price from John & Co. of Agra, an iron water tank gifted by Vice Chairman W. W. Johnstone, tiles from the Perfect Tile Company of Jubbalpore, fifty pounds of tea from J. G. Greensill of Palanpore, Kangra, and so on. In the winter of 1908, Mr T. J. Sullivan gave the children an altogether unexpected but delightful treat by inviting them to High Tea at the toniest hotel in town — The Savoy — and gave them Re. 1 each too!

Quiet, good work at a steady pace began to reflect in better examination results, better placements for those leaving school and more students opting for the High School Examination. However, a stern, almost austere streak was evident in the rules and regulations — some laid down and others unstated but nevertheless understood. Reading novels was prohibited, so was dancing. Teachers were not encouraged to go dancing, watch theatricals or go to the Rink or to any of the public halls in town. Games of chance were not allowed during the Fancy Fair. It was mandatory for all pupils and teachers to attend Bible class and daily worship.

Yet, the School tried, to the best of its abilities, to organise whatever amenities it could. *Dak gharries* or *tongas* would be available at the railhead at Saharanpur when children arrived from their homes in the first week of April and hired coolies and *dandies* would ferry luggage to and from the School. Children continued to be well, though plainly, fed throughout the School year. Gifts of clothing ensured they stayed warm and well-covered in the harsh winters and the kindness of friends and strangers ensured they invariably had a good time at Christmas with some pocket money for little treats over New Year. Just before the end of the School year, cash prizes would be given for 'Improvement' and 'Perseverance' as well as Special Prizes for Needlework, Music, Household Duties, Monitress Duties, Good Conduct, Lady-like Deportment and Good Controlling Influence.

By the year 1905, the School had adopted 'Excelsior' as its motto (inspired by the poem of the same name by H. W. Longfellow) and while the School emblem showed a flag bearing the motto, it was not atop a pyramid of rocks. A Founders' Day Programme, celebrated on 3 October 1905, bears the School motto and emblem along with a list of the day's events.

In the earthquake of April 1905 the property called Constantia suffered terrible damage and became uninhabitable.[4] But the following year started on a promising note: the School boasted 129

EXCELSIOR.

The School's motto, Excelsior, was inspired by a poem by H. W. Longfellow.

[4] Oddly enough, the Logbook entry for this period clearly states that Constantia was burned down on 22 August 1896 in an act of arson; it goes on to state that a reward of Rs. 100 was offered to find the culprit. The discrepancy of date and cause of its devastation between the Minutes of the Managing Committee Meeting and the Principal's Report is perplexing, to say the least.

children on its rolls, the highest so far; the Government granted a fund of Rs. 35,000 to build a new fire-proof steel-frame building in its place to accommodate 40 boys and half-a-dozen teachers as well as the Principal and his family; and the Railways agreed to carry the construction material from Bombay at reduced freight charges, thus saving the School thousands of rupees. Till the new building came up, the neighboring building called Monte Cristo was hired for Rs. 1,200.

Facing page: Old Mussoorie and Landour. Below: Bobby Sahib ka Hotel being demolished to pave the way for the Major Hart Memorial Block, Wynberg (next page).

The School management hoped that the new steel building would be a 'good advertisement for further such buildings in Mussoorie'. What is more, it was now in a position to look ahead with optimism and hope. The increasing numbers of students was both gratifying and reassuring: for, not only was the school being better known and appreciated, it was evidently meeting a very real need. What is more, in the year 1906, the School was registered as a High

School and sent three pupils for the High School examination. The Teacher's Training Class, begun in 1905 with three pupils, was coming along satisfactorily. The feeling of well-being, of being blessed, permeated the School as its pupils and staff proved themselves worthy of the many gifts of kindness that came their way: 211 and a quarter yards of flannelette sent free of charge by the Allen family of Cawnpore (a family that would play a prominent part in the School's fortunes in the years to come); a gift of Rs. 20,000 by a Mussoorie resident for rebuilding Constantia; gratis drill instructions from the Royal Welsh Fusiliers Regiment at Agra; a concert by the First Royal Dragoons to raise funds, and much else besides.

As the School recorded its twentieth year and the occasion to look back presented itself, the Chairman, J. F. T. Hallowes, conceded that the history of an institution such as the Wynberg Homes was

like the life of an average human being where light and shade follow each other. At the same time, he was anxious that the methods and procedures adopted by the School should 'commend themselves to God'. For, as he wrote in his Annual Remarks for 1908:

> In order to approve ourselves constantly to Him, we would seek, more and more, to steep the whole of our enterprise in prayer; we would realise even more vividly, that the children we receive, and train, are a solemn trust from Him, and we would raise the necessary funds in ways, which are certain to secure the Divine approval. It is the duty of Institutions, not only to make a conscience of spending their money, which is generally admitted, but of raising it, which is also allowed, tho' perhaps not so generally.

The chief reason for the well-being — financial, moral and educational — of the institution he helmed was, according to Hallowes, the 'absence of the cold hand of officialism'. It was left to the judgement of the Managing Committee how best to be 'father to the fatherless' and 'cause the widows heart to sing for joy'. With education being a Provincial rather than Central matter, it was left to the discretion of the Provincial Government to look into the functioning of partly-aided schools such as the one at Wynberg. And the Government of the United Provinces, in its wisdom, had decided to allow the schools set up by Anglo-Indians for Anglo-Indians to run with minimal interference. In the next chapter, we shall see how this happy state of affairs was to last for another two decades as the Wynberg Homes continued to provide a safe haven, away from the tides and currents that hurtled the rest of the country towards the most cataclysmic event of the century, namely, the partition of 1947.

1908-1928

FROM
GRACE TO GLORY
The Years
of Consolidation

Children at play at the Wynberg Homes.

I will do better unto you than at your beginnings.
Ezekiel 36:11

The year 1908 was a trying one for the School: an exceptionally strong gale blew away the entire roof of Cedar Hall, the boys' dormitory, and caused extensive damage to the other school buildings. Once again, friends and well-wishers rose to the occasion and launched donation drives to collect money. Unfortunately, a meagre sum of Rs. 571-12-6 was collected; it was barely one-fourth of the amount needed to cover the cost of repairs. The year also saw the worst water shortage Mussoorie had yet seen. Water had to be carried by hand from the stream below and an additional sum had to be set aside for porters. To make matters worse, the number of paying students dwindled. Already, the amount of fees received in the past year had been insufficient to cover the mounting costs of teachers' salaries, wages of domestic staff, fuel, lighting, food, etc. Of the 83 boarders on roll in 1908, 22 were entirely free

scholars; 19 paid a fee between Rs. 5 and Rs. 10; 27 paid between Rs. 15 and Rs. 20; and 9 between Rs. 20 and Rs. 25. Six of the day scholars paid Rs. 5 and three were free. This worked out to a bare Rs. 11 and six annas per pupil — far, far below what the School actually spent on feeding and housing each child! The School Secretary, Charles E. Norris, went on a tour to raise funds and spread awareness about the School and its activities through a series of Lantern Lectures in different cities. The railways helped by subsidising the cost of travel.

As the School struggled with its finances, it was blessed in other ways, most notably with trained and dedicated teachers who would, in the years to come, make a noticeable difference in not merely the quality of teaching but its reflection in better examination results. Miss Laplace returned with a Teacher's Diploma from Bedford College, London. Miss Maud Powell, daughter of the Powell family that owned Seven Oaks near Wynberg, joined the School with a Masters from Edinburgh University. The other teachers, too, were trained, some having been educated at Calcutta, Jubbalpore, Lucknow, etc. and a few at the teacher's training school at Woodstock, or as in the case of Miss E. Law, from St. Bede's. Mrs West's second daughter, Daisy West, joined the School to teach Classes VII and VIII, and a certain Miss Chew was employed to teach typing and shorthand.

In keeping with the Government's Code for European Schools, increasing emphasis began to be given on practical training: nursing, cooking, domestic economy as well as dressmaking. In fact, students could opt for Cooking, Dressmaking, Shorthand and Typing instead of any three 'regular' subjects for the Middle School Examination. Many girls chose these classes and did exceptionally well, landing jobs soon after their examinations.[1] In fact, such was

[1] It must be remembered that Anglo-Indian women comprised 80 per cent of India's nursing services — both military and civilian — right up till Independence. The high standards of the Indian nursing services were comparable with any in the western world.

the prowess of the Cookery Class that it began to take in small orders for afternoon teas turning out perfectly produced cakes, biscuits, sweets, etc. and making a small profit for the School. In 1908, of the 15 pupils taking piano classes, one was presented for the Trinity College Junior Music Examination; she passed. A junior Y.W.C.A. was started in the same year by the energetic Miss Curtis whose 'pleasing personality, musical gifts, and noble Christian character' left a strong impression on the girls. On the last Friday of every month, a Literary Exercise would be held at Meakin Hall where members of the School staff as well as friends from outside attended. These co-curricular activities leavened the School's formal classroom teaching and added substantially to the over-all development of the students.

While the small community at Wynberg plodded steadily on, piling one modest accomplishment over another, building firm

Emphasis was given to practical training such as nursing and cooking in keeping with the Government's Code for European Schools.

Old Mussoorie bus terminal.

foundations for the better days that waited round the corner, it held itself aloof from the gay goings-on in the city. Since 'unofficial' Mussoorie had none of the strict, codified protocol-driven socialising of the official summer capital, Shimla, those who came here let their hair down with a vengeance. Afternoon teas, balls, fancy dress parties, garden parties, fetes, fancy bazars — not to mention trysts and liaisons — were held at a hectic pace all through the 'season' with no thought other than a hedonistic indulgence in pure, unadulterated pleasure. The city's first amusement hall, the Rink, had been built by Joseph Miller in 1890; soon, it emerged as the venue of many an exciting venture. In fact, as early as 22 October 1884, the venerable *Statesman* had

View of the Wynberg Homes.

published the shocking news of a lady standing up on a chair and auctioning kisses for Rs. 5 at a fancy bazar! Local newspapers, such as *The Hills, The Advertiser, The Mussoorie Times, The Beacon, The Echo*, etc. carried titillating news and salacious gossip of the many goings-on among the bold and the beautiful who 'came up'.

Already, travel to Mussoorie had been facilitated by the opening of the Haridwar-Dehradun railway line in 1901. To cater to the needs of the rich and famous, the elegant Savoy Hotel was established in 1902, and a year later the St Mary's Cottage Hospital began to take care of medical eventualities. In 1905, the city was given a major overhaul to coincide with the visit of Her Royal Highness the Princess of Wales (later Queen Mary) who stayed at the Charleville Hotel (now the Lal Bahadur Shastri National Academy of Administration for civil servants). Yet another feather in Mussoorie's already-famous cap was added with the arrival of electricity. Lights were switched on for the first time on Empire Day, 24 May 1909, though it was a while before electrification reached every nook and corner of the station. It would be four years later, on 14 April, 1913, that electric lights were used at the Wynberg School.

They that know the Lord shall do exploits.
Daniel 11:32

Mr J. Murray, Inspector of European Schools for the United Provinces, in submitting his report for the year 1911, strongly advised the Managing Committee of the perils of pauperisation, and the need to 'make the most careful enquiry regarding every application for reduced rates and the granting of such applications only in thoroughly deserving cases. Care in this matter,' he cautioned, 'may reduce the enrolments, but that is as it should be.' Coupled with the most rigorous enquiry into the merits of each free case, certain other procedures were laid down, such as a certificate from the District Magistrate that the family was indeed indigent and that the parent(s) could not afford the school fee. Applications that seemed genuine or came highly recommended received the fullest consideration with urgent or special cases receiving immediate attention. Moreover, the School prided itself on its laid-down policy: *'No destitute orphan is ever refused.'* In cases where the parent could afford even a part of the fee, the School insisted that at least an attempt be made towards paying some part of the School expenses. The parents or guardians were also encouraged to send the School outfits and items of clothing if not all at once, then make up the 'deficiencies monthly to complete the list'.

Within the larger category of 'freeships', the Managing Committee also made certain other distinctions that would help them serve the most needy:

- Real Orphans, whose both parents were dead, and were thus entirely dependent on the School for fee, board, lodging and any other incidentals that might crop up during the School year;

- Real Orphans, whose both parents were dead, but were partly supported by small subscriptions, not exceeding Rs. 10 per month each, the amount being paid by benevolent patrons;

- Orphans, whose father was dead but mother alive, but were destitute and therefore dependent on the School; and

- Pupils whose parents or guardians paid Rs. 10 on an average, depending on their means.

As the School inched towards its Silver Jubilee, several small changes, accumulating over the years, began to reveal themself. The Annual Report for 1913 showed a curious change of nomenclature. The School that had hitherto been known as the Christian Training School and Orphanage was now being called the Wynberg School and Orphanage. What is more, it could now boast of some very eminent persons on its Managing Committee. His Excellency, the Right Hon'ble Charles Baron Hardinge of Penhurst was its Chief

1912

Remarks heard whilst going round collecting money for Wynberg —

That Wynberg Committee should not have refused the money last year — Some very indignant.

— That Wynberg paid some of the teachers too high a Salary — as far as 100£!

3 — That Miss Wyckoff ought to go round making friends for Wynberg.

4 — That Miss Wyckoff should go round herself! to collect money for the School and not get another to do so —

5 — That too many Teachers are engaged in Wynberg.

6 — That a secretary should not be kept. Several other Schools have no secretary.

7 — Why is Wynberg needing money, did'nt they have a Fancy Sale lately?

That it is a mistake to get the girls to cook, serve at table, and sweep, no wonder the School has reduced to nearly half the numbers — Had the School been started on those lines it would have been different — only cooking lessons should be given.

Remarks heard while collecting money for Wynberg, 1912.

9 – That a music teacher is not necessary since the parents cannot afford even the tuition fees –

10 – One person, especially, very much offended, because of clothes sent to Wynberg for the children, have been sold to Kabāris in the bazaar, and seen there by the person who sent the clothes.

11 – Its not enough that a canvasser should have been sent round, but now Mrs Alfred Powell is going round asking for Umbrellas for Wynberg!

12 – Why should there be 2 matrons and a housekeeper?

13 – Why are you canvassing is it not a Govt: aided school?

Collected Rs 252 by Mrs Beck

Patron. Other patrons included: His Honour Sir James Meston, the Hon'ble Sir Harcourt Butler, Lt-General Sir Robert Scallon and the Hon'ble J. H. Abbott. In the Chairman's Report for 1913, Reverend Hallowes wrote:

> By the kindness of Members of our Committee we have a new roadway, a new playground, and our old playground has the beginnings of a Gymnasium with swings, seesaw and a giant stride.

While the Board of Management continued to have old faithfuls such as Reverend J. F. T. Hallowes and W. W. Johnstone who served as Vice-Chairman, two new names became associated with the School: Henry Deacon Allen and his wife Gertrude Petronella (Nella). The story of Henry Allen's association with Wynberg is an interesting one; it also shows how seemingly serendipitous events happen with a gentle nudge from the Almighty. Allen (born on 13 September 1864), the second son of Sir George Allen, the co-founder and owner of Cooper Allen in Cawnpore as well as owner of the Cawnpore Woollen Mills,[2] happened to drop by at the School while on holiday in Mussoorie. Extremely impressed by the work being done and also keenly aware of the need for institutions such as the Wynberg Homes, Allen began to take an active interest in the School and took to dropping by every alternate Tuesday in 1913 to take regular classes; his lessons from the life of Joseph proved to be helpful and instructive for his pupils. As his involvement with the school grew, his role became a more structured one; by 1917 he was Vice-Chairman and a year later Chairman. His association with the School remained a long and fruitful one.

[2] The Cawnpore Woollen Mills were set up in 1876 by five residents of Cawnpore, namely, George Allen, W. E. Cooper, Bevan Petman, Gavin S. Jones and Dr Condon (the same Brigade Surgeon who was also among the four founder-members of the Christian Training School and Orphanage at Mussoorie). The mill was initially set up for the manufacture, chiefly, of army blankets; later it began producing felt, flannel and other woollen items. We have seen in Chapter One how the Cawnpore Woollen Mills had sent several yards of flannelette to the school free of charge. In later years, it became known by the brand Lal Imli.

He who gives a child a treat
Makes joy-bells ring in Heaven's street
And he who gives a child a home
Builds palaces in Kingdom Come.

John Masefield

By the turn of the century, a steady stream of visitors had begun to find their way to Wynberg. There were, of course, the good people of Mussoorie who continued to take an active interest in the School — the Jahans, Powells, Diamantopoulos, Collins, Vansittarts, James, Christies, among others. Possibly as a result of the tours undertaken by the School Secretary or the vast numbers of printed Prospectuses sent out annually, awareness about the School was indeed reaching far and wide. Spurred by curiosity about this home in the hills for the most disenfranchised and disempowered of God's own children, many well-meaning visitors dropped by. Miss Wise, Travelling Secretary of the Home Missionary Society of India, came to deliver a lecture in 1913, as did Mr Archibald of the Children's Mission, Mr Butler of the Bible Society and Dr Gilmore-Carter who gave a Lantern Lecture. On 11 July 1913 the Hon'ble Mr Abbott and his sister, Mrs Newman of Jhansi — both long-time benefactors of the School — came up. What is more, Mr Abbott took the children for a special treat at the Picture Palace. Other little treats were lined up with unfailing regularity: a picnic at the airfield organised by Mrs Gordon whose expenses were defrayed from the money sent though Mr Oakden from the Lady Hardinge Fund; pocket money for each child given by the ever-thoughtful Mrs Alfred Powell at the Union Church Fancy Fair; Mrs Skinner who sent money for treats; and prize money for the Annual Day prizes given by Mr Arthur Powell. In 1913, a windfall, called the Emile Legacy, brought the handsome amount of Rs. 5,000 into the School's kitty. In 1914, 'a friend' sent Rs. 300 with the express purpose of installing a telephone connection;

five connections were put in place, thus connecting the different sections of the School.

As the imminent outbreak of the First World War threatened to plunge the world in turmoil, the School at Wynberg remained an oasis of calm. The Principal's Report for the year 1913 noted with quiet satisfaction 'how the dews of heaven have fallen thick in blessing upon us all along the way and our hearts are filled with gratitude'. Miss Wyckoff, the Lady Principal, spelt out the School's agenda in the years ahead thus:

> It is our ambition, as soon as our funds will allow, to take in at least two per cent of the 7,000 Anglo-Indian children in India growing up without any educational advantages whatever. If neglected now, these children will become a menace to society, whereas if Wynberg, Kalimpong, Coonoor, and similar Schools can take them in hand at once, they can be trained to become good, honest, worthy citizens — a source of strength to the Empire, and we fondly hope, by the blessing of God, the means of bringing India to Christ. This is God's economy. Is it not an honour to be co-workers with him in such a cause? We want gifts, but above all, we want prayers for Wynberg.

The Bishop of Lucknow, stressing the interdenominational nature of the School and the willingness of the School Committee to respect the religious antecedents of the children under its care, appealed to all sections of the Christian community in India to come forward and help in this 'difficult but important work'. He even circulated an Appeal in the April 1914 issue of the *Lucknow Diocesan Chronicle* — an appeal that was reprinted in the *Mussoorie Times* — soliciting help and inviting people to visit the School and see with their own eyes the work being done at Wynberg. With children from as far north as Rawalpindi and as far south as Secunderabad, as well as large numbers of children from cities as far apart as Lucknow and Calcutta, evidently the School — far from being a provincial outpost — was slowly acquiring a pan-Indian outlook.

And so life continued on an even keel. The School continued to prove its usefulness and maintain its claim on the public for help and support. A Wynberg Girl, Kathleen Russell, won a prize for the best essay on 'What Kind of a Girl Needs India' organised by the *Home Missionary Magazine*. Distinguished visitors continued to wind their way to Wynberg, the most notable being Sir James Meston, Lieutenant-Governor of the United Provinces who came in July 1915, followed in October 1915 by the Bishop of Lucknow.

Possibly the only fall-out of the war clouds that loomed over much of the western world was a drop in subscriptions and donations as any spare funds, however meagre, went towards the War Effort. The School also suffered a dip in the Government's Grant-in-Aid as money had to be diverted to the trenches. The School tightened its belt, strengthened its resolve and soldiered on. Despite its own mounting expenses, it managed to make a contribution to the Red Cross Society. What was especially heartening was the children's request to give away their annual prize money to the soldiers' fund. Only a few stray references to the war that engulfed the world arena are to be found among the School's records. For instance, W. W. Johnstone resigned as Vice-Chairman owing to his absence from Mussoorie on War Service, and in 1917 Mr Norris, the Secretary, received an Officer's Commission in a Labour Corps and left on Military Duty.[3]

[3] The military potential of the Anglo-Indian community had long been the subject of debate. Till 1791, Anglo-Indians were freely admitted into the British Army but in an order published in the *Calcutta Gazette* of 14 June 1792, 'persons of Indian extraction were precluded from employment as officers in the Civil, Military or Marine Services of the East India Company and by 1808 Anglo-Indians, of all ranks, were discharged from the British Army. The Mutiny of 1857 brought belated recognition of the importance of having Anglo-Indians in the armed forces. At a meeting of the Anglo-Indian Association in Calcutta in 1885, a resolution was passed to write to the Government to raise an Anglo-Indian regiment. When the First World War was declared on 5 August 1914, J. H. Abbott, President-in-Chief of the Anglo-Indian Empire League, wired to the Commander-in-Chief offering to raise an Anglo-Indian regiment for service abroad as well as a corps of women nurses. The offer was declined. But as the War dragged on, the British Army, on 15 March 1916 sanctioned the raising of an Anglo-Indian Force as an integral part of the British Army. During these two years that the War ravaged Europe and the Middle East, approximately 8,000 Anglo-Indians had joined various British units as Europeans. Those who didn't see active combat, joined as gym instructors or as signal and gunnery instructors. By 1916, two field troops of Cavalry, one section of Field Artillery and 16 platoons of Infantry were raised. Of these, the Anglo-Indian Battery, stationed at Jhansi and attached to the 77th Royal Field Artillery, was the most popular choice for recruitment. Later, the Indian Defence Force (also known as the Auxiliary Force) was drawn almost entirely from the Anglo-Indian community.

However, several small changes did creep up on account of the War and caught the School unawares, for instance, galloping inflation pushed prices of all essential commodities sky high. By 1918, it cost Rs. 240 to feed, clothe and educate one destitute child for one year instead of the Rs. 200 of the previous year. The School decided to put collection boxes in churches, hotels and other prominent locations with 'Wynberg Homes' written in big, bold letters. To further add to the financial woes, the School building was found to be 'decidedly unsafe' by the Inspector of Schools. According to the rules and regulations, the School was not eligible for any government help for building purposes unless it could furnish, from its own resources, at least one-third of the total cost. Once again, despite the trying circumstances, the School sent out appeals for help; this time mincing no words: '...every rupee you can kindly give or collect for us on this account enables us to earn another two rupees from the Government.' The School applied for a Special Building Grant of Rs. 30,000 in 1917 but was turned down due to other pressing demands on the Provincial Government as it coped with austerity measures.

A sad blow was dealt by the passing away of the School Chairman, Rev J. F. T. Hallowes, who died on 20 December 1917 at Mathura (or Muttra as it was then spelt) where he was conducting a 'Special Mission' in an Indian Christian orphanage. Writing the Foreword in his stead in the year 1918, H. D. Allen stressed the need for a School such as the one at Wynberg given the mayhem unleashed by the War:

> The children of the present will become the citizens of the future, and they must be so trained as to inherit the glorious Empire for which their fathers are fighting and dying. Here is valuable 'war work' to be done in this country, work which, if well done, will have far reaching and imperishable results, but we need your practical help in saving children and training them for the best service of the Empire.

Wynberg School & Orphanage.

CHIEF PATRON:

His Excellency the Right Hon'ble CHARLES BARON HARDINGE OF PENSHURST, P.C., G.C.B., G.M.S.I., G.M.I.E., G.C.M.G., G.C.V.O., I.S.O.

PATRONS:

His Honour Sir JAMES MESTON, K.C.S.I.
The Hon'ble Sir HARCOURT BUTLER, K.C.S.I., C.I.E.

Lieut.-General Sir ROBERT SCALLON, K.C.B., K.C.I.E., D.S.O., A.D.C.
The Hon'ble Mr. J. H. ABBOTT.

Mussoorie, U. P.

191

I, Nella Allen of Mussoorie, being a member of the Board of Management of the above Insti- -tution and entitled to vote, hereby appoint Henry Deacon Allen of Cawnpore as my prixy to vote for me and on my behalf at the General Meeting of the C.T.S. & O. Association to be held on Wednesday, the 19th. July 1916 at 4-30 p.m. and at any adjourne- -ment or adjournements thereof.

As witness my hand this 18th day of July 1916.

Signed by the said
Nella Allen
in the presence of
M.A. Benskin

N.B. The stamp should be cancelled by writing the signature and date across it.

Attention to the Anglo-Indian community came from another, altogether unexpected, quarter. An article published in the *Englishman*, and reprinted in the *Pioneer* dated 1 August 1917, drew attention to the physique of members of this community. The article (below) deserves to be reproduced in its entirety.

Even in the absence of concrete figures, the Managing Committee at Wynberg Homes had, virtually from the School's inception given a great deal of importance to physical education. In fact, in inviting visitors, the School authorities wished to show, in the words of Henry Allen, the 'changes it is possible to effect in

Physique of Anglo-Indians

Many before the War had a suspicion that the average Anglo-Indian was far below the average European in physique but it was not till recruiting for the Anglo-Indian Force was in full swing that this suspicion was turned to absolute certainty. And of course, if the men are below the recognised standard in physical development, it stands to reason that the boys also are of inferior build. A writer in the "Boys Scouts' Gazette of India" brings this point out painfully in figures of measurements of some London and some Indian boys of all ages and comes to the conclusion that the result is on average that a boy of 15 in India equals a boy of 13½ at Home, a boy of 14 in India equals a boy of 12½ at Home…There are of course, many causes that lead to this result, *e.g.*, poverty, early marriages, neglect of home hygiene, and, no matter what may be attempted to uplift the community intellectually, it is here that the evil lies. It is here that the root cause of the general backwardness of Anglo-India is to be found. It is here that those interested in the community will find the most important problem awaiting a solution. How is this deterioration in physical development to be overcome? It is imperative that the question be tackled in no half-hearted spirit for without healthy and fully-developed bodies how can Anglo-Indians be expected to have healthy brains and healthy minds? To fill the place in India that is theirs, to be considered of some value to the State, to be acknowledged by other communities as opponents not to be despised, all these are at stake and the community in general, not one or two isolated members, must give this question of physique earnest consideration, and all unite in taking measures to make the members of future generations of a better build and greater stamina.

poor children from the plains during the most impressionable years of their growth with the aid and advantages of healthy surroundings, good plain food, regular living, judicious discipline, and European supervision and influences'.

Reading the Minutes of the Managing Committee meetings alongside the Annual Reports of the Chairman and Principal/ Supervisor are illuminating, for what is left out in one is, inadvertently, picked up in the other. For instance, the Minutes reveal that the Wynberg School was affiliated with the St Andrew's school and orphanage at Kalimpong in a loose, semi-official way. For instance, after a certain age boys would be transferred to Kalimpong for further studies and vocational training. Or, in some cases, the Home Missionary Society of India would be asked to pitch in with help — as the case of illness of some child on the 'free list'. These Minutes also reveal that in 1913 a resolution was passed to limit the 'free list' to 20, including the five 'Foy Scholars', that is, those children who received a free scholarship in memory of the Founder-Chairman, Arthur Foy. The Managing Committee also resolved, on 18 August 1913, that no Indian children be admitted either as boarders or day scholars. In one instance, in 1914, when upon admission it was realised that the father of two students was Indian, he was asked to remove his wards.

By 1917, the School had substantially increased its enrolments; it now had 160 boarders and 35 day scholars with 26 free children and 130 on reduced fees. All along, the School had done yeoman's service for needy girls; boys, on the other hand, had been somewhat overlooked. While the School at Wynberg took in girls of all ages, the age limit for boys had been set at 12 as, it was felt, teenage boys could not be satisfactorily controlled by lady teachers. At the same time, both the teachers and administrators felt the urgent need for a separate school for senior boys with a competent staff of masters who would take over, from the lady teachers in the junior wing, the charge of educating the older boys. Educated with the girls till the junior classes, the boys would either be sent to Kalimpong after the age of 12 or to the Philander Smith College in Mussoorie. However, a problem arose when the Philander Smith College was transferred to Nainital and the Kalimpong Homes conveyed their inability to take in any more boarders. What was to be done with these boys? Not old enough to be turned out into an uncaring world, nor educated enough to fend for themselves, they needed institutional help and the benefits of a formal, structured education. Something had to be done.

In December 1918, H. D. Allen, by now the Chairman of the School, noted how the War had changed many things; it had, most importantly changed the way of *seeing* the world:

> The war has opened our eyes to many things, and especially to the importance of the moral base of life. With the example of Germany before us we must know by this time that unless education has a sound moral base we are more likely than not to produce a race that is clever in everything save the thing that matters — character.

Character building, all along the corner stone of education at Wynberg, was buttressed with the belief that character must be formed and developed on practical Christian lines. Coupled with this was a keen sense of the exigencies of the time. The end of the war and the terrible toll of human life had made the European community in India apprehensive of what the future might hold. It had left in its wake widespread unemployment, galloping inflation, thousands of injured or crippled young men, countless widows and orphans. The children of the present, many who had precious little of their own, would be the future citizens of the world; their mind, body and spirit needed the right sustenance to grow on wholesome lines. A school in the hills, an environment far removed from deleterious influences, a healthy combination of secular and religious training — these were the demands of the age.

Unfortunately, Henry Deacon Allen died on 25 January 1919 and did not live to see the Wynberg Homes keep their tryst with destiny. His wife, Nella, donated the substantial sum of Rs. 90,000 for the new boys' school, and, even though she went away to England with her four children, continued to return to India every year for the next forty years.

He who helped us hitherto, will help us all our journey through.

Samuel 7:12

Facing page: Henry Allen Memorial Boys' School, main building.

Just when the school was looking for a separate building to house the older boys, a neighbouring property happened to come into the market. What is more it was being offered to the School Committee on favourable terms. Originally owned by John Edward Powell, it was bequeathed to his daughter, Vida Harriet Powell and sold to the Wynberg Homes Society in November 1919 for a sum of Rs. 35,000. This was the Bala Hissar Estate, home of the exiled Afghan Amir Dost Mohammad during his internment in 1842. Known for generations as 'Bala', this was bought in 1919 and became the Henry Allen Memorial Boys' School. Named after the man who had most passionately espoused the cause of a separate senior school for boys and who had, tragically, not lived to see it come to fruition, it began life with 31 boys who had been 'transferred' from Wynberg. An endowment of Rs. 15,000 from an anonymous friend eased the birth pangs of this new school born of fierce hopes and modest means.

In May 1919 the U.P. Government sanctioned a grant of Rs. 5,870 for a much-needed hospital building with an isolation ward for infectious cases. One-third of the estimated cost of long-awaited renovations could now come from the European Schools Improvement Association.

A makeshift hall (with a corrugated iron roof) doubled up as a refectory, study-room and prayer hall. Work began on a playground and the teaching of boys from Standard IV to Junior Cambridge began under the guidance of Mr Brown. By 1922, in its third year, the Henry Allen Memorial Boys' School, also occasionally called the Wynberg Boys' School, had 58 boarders. With the Rev A. T. Roberts as Principal, it strove valiantly to keep afloat; its mission, at this stage of its infancy, was to be 'as well known and almost as big as the Wynberg School'.

The Wynberg family received a boost with the arrival of Major F. W. Hart, a long-time member of the staff at the Thomason Engineering College at Roorkee and formerly of the 60th King's Royal Rifles, who took over as Superintendent of both Schools in April 1923. P. M Buck, Chairman of the Board of Management, noted his 'marked business ability, and experience with students, and peculiar tact, and sane religious character, and kindly spirit' that combined to make him admirably suited to the job of running the two schools at Wynberg. Major Hart brought an enlightened liberalism to the running of the boys' school. Occasional lectures on photography, politics, travel, and world affairs began to be delivered with unfailing regularity by distinguished speakers. Inter-school matches in hockey, football and boxing, were held with Woodlands and Oak Grove Schools. Picnics and concerts were jointly organised with the Wynberg girls.

Major Hart's ceaseless devotion soon paid rich dividends. The boys' school, so far a part of the girls' school, was recognised by the government in 1924 as a separate entity. Also, prudent investments ensured that the School's financial condition was stable after many years in the doldrums. Despite the post-war depression in trade and the subsequent fall in donations, expenditure was less than income. With soaring unemployment and poverty among the domiciled community, there was the need — more than ever before — of boarding schools that provided a sound education at modest cost. Of the 210 boarders on roll, the majority could not afford the low fees. The first Indian students were admitted in 1924 on full fee. The boys were divided, for the purpose of games, into four houses, namely, Allen, Johnstone, Roberts and Hart. The 'Big Sister' (Wynberg), choosing to take a leaf from the book of the 'Little Brother' (Bala Hissar), followed suit; it grouped the students into four Houses named after those who had played a crucial role in the inception and development of the School, namely, Foy, Powell, West and Allen. Each House had a Prefect and a distinctive colour.

Notes of the proceedings of the Special Thanksgiving Service held at Wynberg on the 8th October 1926.

The following members of the Committee were present, Messrs. F.W.Roberts, J.T.Robertson, A.E.Hart, A.L.Parker & F.W.Hart; Mrs. Hooper, Miss Phillips; Mrs. Hart, Head Mistress of Wynberg and Mr. McIntosh, Head Master of the Boys' School, and other friends were present on the dais.

When all had taken their places the Hymn "O God our help in ages past" was sung. The Superintendent then gave a short address first on the history of the Wynberg Homes making special allusion to those who had done much in establishing the schools and secondly on the history of the Homes for the past few years giving figures of the debt which has now been cleared off.

During the course of his address he mentioned that it was recorded in one of the minute books that the first meeting to inaugurate the Christian Training School and Orphanage was held at Cawnpore on the 5th October 1887 at the instance of Mr. Arthur Foy of that place. The inception of the scheme was his, and he was soon afterwards joined by Mr. Alfred Powell of Sevenoaks Mussoorie, who was known as a lover of children, and by Dr. Condon of Cawnpore Others have from time to time helped in the work, but the above named three were the actual founders as far as is known. The Powell family have in one way and another maintained their connection with the institution ever since.

He went on to say that the school was first opened in Jabr Khet in 1888 with 2 children, and later moved to South Hill, then Dunedin, then Wolfsburn, and found its permanent home in Wynberg in 1893. It has literally been through fire and earthquake, having been burnt out in Jabr Khet at an early stage of its existence, and the old Constantia building was destroyed by earthquake, prior to the present building being erected. Although the institution has suffered many vicissitudes the hand of God in blessing has been over it all along.

Mrs. West, mother of Mrs. Johnstone of Whytbank Castle,- whose husband has been longest on the Board of Management among present members - was the first Lady Principal, from 1889 to the date of her death in 1895.

It was in 1904 that Mr. & Mrs. H.D.Allen joined the Board of Management and from that time until his death in 1919 Mr. Allen worked incessantly for the good of Wynberg. At a very early stage in his connection with the school he saw the necessity of founding a boys' school, as his heart used to ache when he saw boys leaving Wynberg at the age of 11 or 12, with no prospect of getting further education, unless they went to St. Fidelis, where many actually found their way. Mrs. Allen's connection has been maintained to the present date and it is largely due to her generosity, under the guiding hand of God, that we are here today to celebrate our freedom from debt.

Notes of the proceedings during special Thanksgiving Service held at Wynberg on 8 October 1926.

House Logos of Henry Allen Memorial Boys' School.
Top: Hart House, Red.
Above: Condon House, Green.

The Allen family's unstinting help did not end with the large one-time donation of Rs. 90,000 — which was nothing short of a king's ransom in the 1919s; Mrs Allen continued to send thoughtful gifts, such as a set of *The Child's Book of Knowledge* as well as books and pictures for the Boys' School. She would also send, year after year, substantial sums of money from the sales of work which she would hold at her house in Bath, as well as contribution to the stalls at the Wynberg Sale of Work in Mussoorie.

The year 1926 proved to be the financially most sound for the School since its birth three decades ago. The Government finally came through with a grant of Rs. 22,500 towards the purchase of a site and construction of buildings for the Boys' School. A grant-in-aid of Rs. 20,000 was promised by the European Schools Improvement Association. At long last, the School was free of debt and ready to begin a new innings where whatever revenue was generated could be ploughed back into the School, thus lessening its dependence on aid and charity.

By 1928, Wynberg had 168 boarders and 25 day scholars, and Allen had 66 boarders and 4 day scholars. The Boys' School earned its stripes, as it were, by being declared a Senior School, whereas the Girls' School continued to send up candidates, successfully one might add, for the Senior Cambridge Examination. Going by the emphasis on education, it would appear that the School authorities were mindful of the glaring unemployment among Anglo-Indians rampant in post-war India. What the community needed, most urgently, was a sound, practical education that would open up avenues in peacetime services that were, for all practical purposes, 'reserved', namely in Railways,

Posts & Telegraphs, Customs, Police and Marines; and for women in Teaching, Nursing and Secretarial services. Also, as the country was rocked by nationwide labour unrest and wildfire workers' strikes all through the late 1920s, the Government increasingly began to rely upon the Anglo-Indian community that manned these vital services. At a time when vital segments of the Indian economy were paralysed by crippling strikes, the country's lifelines — Railways, Posts & Telegraphs, and Customs — were kept alive and functioning due to the tireless devotion of the Anglo-Indians. Schools, such as Wynberg-Allen, were fully aware of the responsibility that rested with them. Every man and woman had to put their shoulder to the wheel.

Top: Roberts House, Blue.
Above: Johnstone House, Yellow.

1928-1948

RIDING
THE TEMPEST
The Years of
Riding High

Sweet Peace, the Gift of God's Love.
Peter Bilhorn

The period between the two World Wars was a time of great social churning and political unrest. Gandhi had launched his first civil disobedience movement in April 1919, the Khilafat Movement had persuaded the Hindus and Muslims of India all through the early-1920s to come together, and by the late 1920s the country was rocked by workers' strikes, especially in the railways and industrial hubs of Calcutta and Kanpur. The tumultuous decade ended with the First Round Table Conference held in London in 1930 amidst clamorous cries for Swaraj or Self Rule; it was a measure of Imperial concern at the rising political discontent and increasingly violent regional movements across India.

Ironically enough, these years were also years of stability and unhindered growth for the two Schools at Wynberg, possibly their finest hour since their conception. Nestled among the tall oaks and deodars, the School buildings provided not merely a safe haven for the flotsam and jetsam that had been tossed on the shores of an unkind sea but also an uncommonly well-appointed space for young minds to grow and evolve. Taken together, the facilities at the newly-renovated buildings at Bala Hissar, and the new buildings in place of Constantia and Cedar Hall as well as the flats and playgrounds for sports, P.E. drills and a variety of outdoor activities were comparable with any among the hill schools of Upper India. As word of the high standard of teaching and the fine results in the examinations spread, more and more paying students began to come in. But, as Major F. W. Hart, the energetic School Supervisor, was at pains to clarify in his Annual Report for the year 1929, the School had not moved away from its initial objective of caring for the needy and the orphan; over 20 per cent of the students were on the Free List, i.e. 62 of 302 Boarders and the numbers would increase if one included those children whose parents paid Rs. 10 or less per month. (Incidentally, the proportion of boys on the Free List at Bala Hissar

Senior girls' drill display, circa 1930 (following page as well).

remained higher than the girls at Wynberg — a trend that was to continue for the next decade or two.) Also, as the Reverend J. Ireland-Hasler, Pastor, Union Church, wrote in his Foreword for the Annual Report for the following year:

> The references to the educational progress of some of the present, as well as some of the past, pupils is a testimony to the work done at the Schools, and, in connection with it one needs to remember that the task of the teachers is often the harder because of the backwardness of not a few of the scholars admitted. The Schools exist not so much to push on the brilliant as to help the average lads and lasses, notably those who have been handicapped at home. And some, too, would be homeless, were it not for this Institution. Its need and its value are attested by the fact that the applications for admission exceed the number of vacancies.

Given the good Junior and Senior Cambridge results, several children won government scholarships for higher education or training. Seeing the overall academic and sporting prowess of the students, parents increasingly began to *choose* to send their wards

to the two schools here. From being a destination where poor or indigent children were packed off by well-meaning guardians, clergymen, and assorted sponsors, Wynberg Homes emerged not as a default option but a destination of choice for many. Paying students came from different parts of the United Provinces, Bengal, Punjab and further afield as well as the Railways which already had its own school, Oak Grove at Jharipani.

By 1930, the first Indian boys and girls were admitted to the Schools despite criticism from some quarters. These children were found 'in general behaviour and diligence' to be 'no whit behind their European schoolfellows'.[1] So much so that for the year 1931, the head girl at Wynberg was an Indian girl! Significantly, the Reverend notes:

> Moreover, the international nature of the Schools would enable them to play an important part in promoting cooperation between the Britisher and Indian *in the after years.* {italics mine}

By 1932, the Prospectus clearly states:

> Children of non-European parentage or descent are admitted according to vacancies available, but invariably on the payment of full fees, and on the distinct understanding that they conform to all Rules of the School, including School Dress. Some knowledge of English is desirable if these children are to fit happily into their new surroundings where English is the language of class-rooms and playgrounds.[2]

---

[1] Beginning with some native Christian, Armenian and Parsi children, gradually Hindu, Muslim and Sikh children too began to be enrolled. They belonged to the emerging Indian middle class and were the wards of either well-to-do doctors, lawyers, entrepreneurs or the landed classes. I found the reference to Dr Sarwat Rahman, a spry 80-year old whom I met in Dehradun; the daughter of a doctor, she took the Cambridge School Exam from Wynberg in 1938 and received a scholarship of Rs. 25 tenable for 18 months for securing the First Place in the Province. Dr Rahman went on to study at the Lady Hardinge Medical College and worked in France for many years before retiring to her ancestral home in Dallanwala, Dehradun.

[2] Two sets of fees began to be charged from 1932; the board and tuition with ordinary school diet was Rs. 39 per month, whereas if a special vegetarian diet was ordered, it worked out to Rs. 45.

The School suffered a setback with the sudden demise, on 22 June 1933, of Major Hart, who served the Schools not merely as Supervisor but as an indefatigable Champion of the Cause. During his ten years of service, he had come to be regarded as a 'Second Founder'. Since his retirement from the Thomason Engineering College at Roorkee, he had worked untiringly not merely for the welfare of the School but also served on various committees as a public-spirited individual. The Wynberg Society responded to this untimely loss of a good and upright man who had joined the Board of Management in 1915 by launching a public appeal to contribute to the Major Hart Memorial Fund. No finer testimony could be paid to the memory of Major Hart, it was unanimously decided, than to remodel the Girls' School buildings at Wynberg with the funds thus collected, as it was a cause dear to the Major's heart. Gratifying commendations of the work undertaken by the Wynberg Society under the supervision of Major Hart came from several notable quarters including Sir Malcolm Hailey, the Governor of United Provinces, Sir Jwala Prasad Srivastava, Minister for Education in the United Provinces and A. H. Mackenzie, Director of Public Instruction of U.P., the latter going so far as to declare: 'Those who help the Society may be certain that every rupee will produce sixteen annas worth of good.'

Facing page: Strong emphasis on sports and regimen from the early days continues as tradition till present times. Left: Staff Room, Major Hart Memorial Block, 1940.

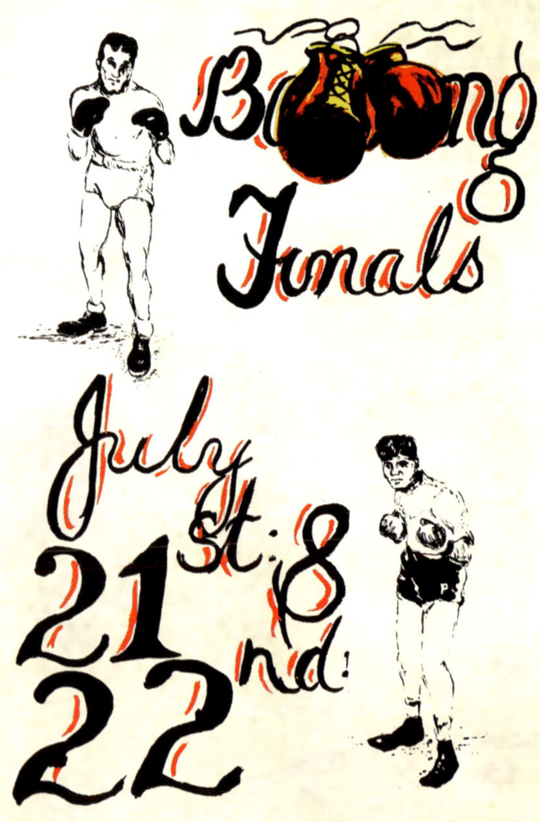

The arrival of H. W. M. Sadleir, B.A. (Cantab) as Principal marked a new chapter for the Schools. Previously an Assistant Master at the Lawrence College, Ghora Gali in Murree he arrived with his wife, a medical doctor who made significant improvements to the health and hygiene at the Wynberg estate. Several firsts were scored during Sadleir's tenure from 1935-1940 when he left as Secretary to the Inter-Provincial Board of Anglo-Indian and European Education: hockey and football matches between the senior boys at Bala and Oak Grove began to be organised; tennis, rifle shooting and polo were added to boxing and other games that were already played with much enthusiasm; the first printed edition of the School Magazine was launched in December 1936; the practice of cutting a Birthday Cake on the School's Founder's Day; and the introduction in 1940 of a venerable institution, well-loved by generations of old boys and girls, namely the Tuck Shop. For the first time, also, importance began to be given to the teaching of Science,

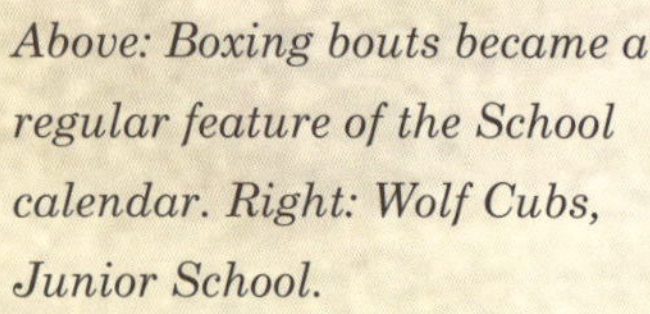

Above: Boxing bouts became a regular feature of the School calendar. Right: Wolf Cubs, Junior School.

Scouts and Cubs.

hitherto neglected due to the lack of equipment and qualified teachers. With the help of a Special Grant from the Department of Education, a Science Laboratory was set up in 1935 and Mr T. J. Brinicombe, an M. Sc. from London University and an Associate of the Royal College of Scientists was hired as Science Master. The new teacher also lent a willing hand with Boy Scouts and Bible Classes.

School Staff, 1940.

While the stream of missionaries continued and included, among others, Reverend N. J. Le Shana, Dr Stanley Jones, Quentin Carr, etc., Sadleir's tenure also saw the arrival of several distinguished visitors including two Governors of the United Provinces: Sir Maurice Hallett, who paid a long-overdue visit in 1937 as the School Patron, followed by Sir Harry Haig who arrived on 14 October 1938 to lay the Foundation Stone of the Major Hart Memorial Building. The decrepit old Bobby's Hotel which had long housed the girls at Wynberg was at long last pulled down and the new building we see today came up. While commending the

project of a new school building as 'one initiated in a spirit of faith and resolution', Sir Harry Haig drew the attention of his young listeners to the sterling qualities of the schools' founders:

> Major Hart's work and character are typical of the spirit which has guided those who have laboured for the upkeep and development of the Wynberg Homes since their inception. I trust that that spirit will prove an example throughout their lives to the boys and girls who derive their education here, and that they will take with them into the world the same ideals of unselfish and persevering service to the community, which has been the inspiration of the founders and makers of Wynberg.

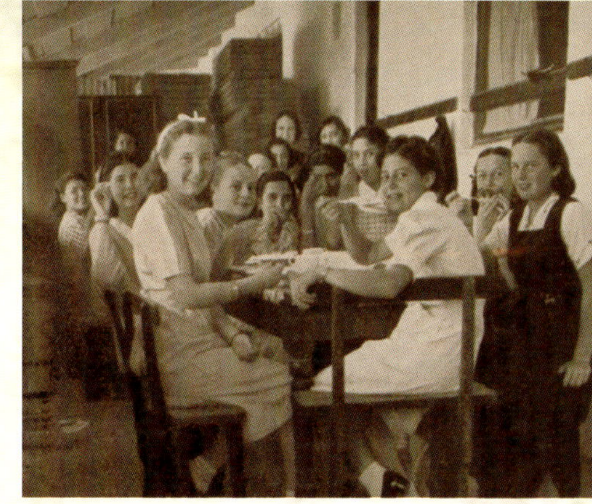

Facing page: Lunch table decorated for Sir Harry Haig's visit. Left: Guard of Honour School A. F. (I) inspected by Sir Harry Haig. Above: Sharing with joy.

The new construction activity at Wynberg comprised the building of a new Assembly Hall, Dining Rooms for girls and staff, Staff Common Room, Dormitories, Staff Quarters, Domestic Science Room, Library and playground at an estimated cost of Rs. 122,073. The greater part of construction was completed at a cost of Rs. 82,000 of which a frugal Rs. 9,000 was given by the Government and the remaining Rs. 73,000 was collected through private contributions. That such a large sum was raised at a time when purse strings were tight and pockets empty as war clouds loomed once again threatening the peace of the realm is a measure of the assiduousness of those who went about collecting funds for so worthy a cause.

Not Alone for Mighty Empire.
William P. Merrill

The Second World War, that had been threatening to upset a tenuous global peace, finally broke out when Germany invaded Poland on 1 September 1939. Britain and the Allied forces once again found themself in the thick of a pitched battle against the massed forces of Fascism and a rising tide of Nazism. Declared a 'total war', that is one which demanded all possible resources — human, financial, scientific, industrial — to be expended only towards the War Effort, education naturally took a back seat. Expecting little or no help from a beleaguered Government, the Schools at Wynberg tightened their belt and soldiered on. Boys and girls continued to be presented for the various annual examinations: the Junior and Senior Cambridge School Certificate, Trinity College of Music Examination for Pianoforte, Violin and Musical Theory, Pitman's for Shorthand and Typing, Royal Drawing Society Examination,

L to R: Sir Maurice Hallet visits the School, 1940; Honouring Sir Maurice Hallet; Inspection of Blue Birds and Cubs.

Mackenzie School Examination in Hygiene and First Aid run by the St. John's Ambulance Association of U.P., and the Essay Competition arranged by the Royal Empire Society (the last being a competition for which entries were received from schools all over the British Empire and for which an Allen boy, John Ledlie, stood sixth and was commended for his essay on 'What Part of the British Empire would you Like to Visit, and Why?').

The Annual Report for 1940 begins thus:

> This is a time of special significance for the Wynberg Homes Society and its Schools. Our Nations and Empire stand at the most critical point of their history. We look back into the past and we bow in gratitude to God for his goodness. We look forward into the future and seek his wisdom and will. Our Schools, too, stand at an important juncture in their history, for in this year falls the JUBILEE of their foundation. We look back into their past and thank God for the way He has planned and guided and fulfilled. We unitedly look forward into the future and again with courage and faith seek His presence and control and blessing.

Clockwise from bottom: Wynberg Guides, 1940; School closing day, 27 November 1940; Allen Staff, 1940.

The School set for itself but one agenda: that of 'sending out continually a stream of healthy, educated, trained, God-fearing youths and maidens to take their place in life and to become worthy and happy citizens of India.' In the very first year of war, three boys left Allen to join the Indian Army Corps of Clerks, two enlisted in the Air Force, one joined the Artillery and another the Royal Indian Navy. Mindful of the trend towards industrialisation (spurred by the War), the School began to give extra emphasis to the science subjects. A measure of the far-sightedness and perspicacity of the School administration is to be a found in a remark such as follows:

> For the moment all our boys are readily absorbed in the vortex created by the War machine. This will not last, however, and our duty is to be prepared.

Top: Alvin Hudson, Royal Corps of Signals. Above: Sqn. Ldr. Ian Loughran, Asian Gliding Record Holder. Below: Dehradun Contingent, A.F.

A modest Jubilee function was organised on Founders' Day with an Address by Rev T. S. Howie, Chairman of the Board and the unveiling by Mr A. E. Hart, who had been the Society's Honorary Treasurer for well over thirty years, of photographs of the Four Founders; these four black and white photographs today hang in the foyer of the Sir Kirby Laing Auditorium. The Prize Money of Rs. 330 — normally distributed as Annual Prizes on Founders' Day — was saved, and upon the request of the students, given towards the War Effort. A sum of Rs. 69 was collected for the Doon Defiant Fund and the British War Service Fund, and other substantial amounts were raised for the Lord Mayor's Fund for Air Raid Victims in London, adding up to Rs. 754. With investments in the Society's Provident Fund and the staff's personal investments another Rs. 15,000 was contributed.

Mrs Alter on Jubilee Founders' Day.

All through the War years, the business of teaching went on seamlessly with an equal emphasis on sports and extra-curricular activities. Matches were won and lost, plays and operettas mounted, debates and elocutions organised along with regular Bible reading classes as well as hiking, camping and scouting activities. Possibly, the one area of School activities that received extra attention was the existing unit of the Detachment. All along, sergeants from the units posted in Dehradun had come up to drill the senior boys at Allen; with the advent of War the parades, held twice weekly, began to be attended with devout fervour. The usual drill was enhanced with 'anti-gas training' with the boys being trained in gas respirators as well as mock drills to check their state of preparedness. The sanctioning of a miniature Range made the cadets adept at rifle shooting, thus winning the 'Viceroy's Cup' in 1940.

Douglas Mackintosh, Royal Air Force.

A fall-out of the rigorous practice received by the boys at Allen was the high enrolment in the War Effort. The School Report for 1940 mentions 30 old boys in the Army and at least two in the Royal Air Force (RAF), and notes: 'Many of these have written, saying their training as members of the School detachment has been of great value in gaining them promotion.' Of these, Pilot Officer Charles Dyson won singular glory for the School when he was awarded the Distinguished Flying Cross for gallantry and distinguished services. Having joined the School in 1921 at the age of seven, Dyson had left in 1930 at 17 years of age and went on to England where he received his commission in the RAF. The Annual Report for 1940 notes with pride how Dyson (grandson of a respected elder of the Anglo-Indian community, J. H. Abbott) established 'a record in the Western Desert by shooting down six

GOVERNOR · UNITED PROVINCES

GOVERNOR'S CAMP,
UNITED PROVINCES.

For fifty years the Wynberg Homes and School at Mussoorie have rendered a great service to the Domiciled and Anglo-Indian Community and have provided suitable education for boys and girls who, for no fault of their own, are in special need of care and assistance. This year the Homes celebrate their Jubilee and it must be the desire of all to congratulate the Society on the work done in the past and to express the wish that the next fifty years may be years of further progress and development.

Governor,
United Provinces.

Top to bottom: Cadet H. T. Menear, winner, Viceroy's Cup; Victor Holmes, 1st Battalion, The Lincolnshire Regiment; Keith Dyson, Royal Fusiliers.

Italian aircraft in 15 minutes.'[3] It goes on to sorrowfully record the 'first death by enemy action of an Allen boy, Charles Fisher, who lost his life in November when the Empire of Bisonon was sunk.'

It must be noted that, as in World War I, this time too almost 75% of the Anglo-Indian community joined the armed forces. Recruitment of Anglo-Indians to the Royal Air Force, which had been abruptly stopped after the last war, was resumed. By the time of the epochal Battle of Britain, between 3000-4000 Anglo-Indians were serving in the R.A.F. Again, as in the previous war, this time the Anglo-Indian women contributed more to the War Effort than all other women from other communities in India, comprising almost 80% of the Women's Auxiliary Corps.[4] As much as 70% of the nurses in the Indian Military Nursing Service and the Auxiliary Nursing Service were Anglo-Indians. They went out into the theatre of war and displayed exemplary courage and devotion to duty. Similarly, the Women's Voluntary Service saw large numbers of volunteers from the Anglo-Indian community.

The peculiar conditions of the War created many job opportunities. The Indian Railways, quite literally the wheels on which India moved its men and materials, had traditionally employed Anglo-Indians in large numbers; the War created an unprecedented strain on existing resources and caused employment at all levels to shoot up. The Civil Disobedience Movement of August 1942, and the disturbances that came in its wake, required intensive patrolling and sentry duties to ensure a smooth and uninterrupted supply chain, especially on the railway track across Upper India that fed the convoy of supplies and troops on their way to Burma. Along with the Railways, the Posts & Telegraphs Department the Ordinance Department, the I.A.C.C. — all battling to cope with the strain on their resources — took in Anglo-Indian girls and boys straight out of schools such as Wynberg-Allen.

[3] Frank Anthony corroborates this account of Dyson's heroic exploits in the Middle East given in the School Annual Report. See: Frank Anthony, *Britain's Betrayal in India* (New Delhi: Allied Publishers, 1969), pp. 130-31.
[4] Ibid., p. 141.

However, the good men and women who comprised the Board of Management at Wynberg Homes were mindful that the War had created unnatural opportunities. They knew that the difficult years of the War would soon be over; their concern was with what lay beyond, after the War had been fought and won:

> Never did problems more acute face a people than today face the people we seek to serve. What will be their position immediately after the War is ended — spiritually, politically, economically, educationally and socially? What is our duty towards our people as we face this unknown future, a future now come very near? How shall we direct all our planning and acting so that this Society may fulfil its mission in Anglo-India's greatest hour of destiny and need? How can we fulfil God's purpose and will, and help our community to fulfil it too in this His challenge? Such are questions upon which the Society increasingly focuses its thought and the solution of which it consecrates itself.

Top to bottom: Mabert King, 2nd Battalion, East Lanes Regiment; Gareth Swarries, Royal Artillery; Stanley Drainsfield, 11 G Battery, Royal Artillery.

With the War in Europe reaching its tentacles into Asia and striking terror along India's eastern arm in Burma, the effects began to be felt among the small community nestling among the mountains of Mussoorie. Government aid — already frugal — was subjected to closer scrutiny. Rationing, food shortages, inflation, rising prices of all consumer goods could not keep pace with the new jobs and increased wages. Already dipping into its reserves to meet the gap between income and expenditure, the Board was forced to hike the fees. The arrival of Rev W. J. Biggs as Principal (on loan from the Baptist Mission) heralded a period of growth and prosperity despite the prevailing financial and political turbulence. The student strength swelled to 373 in 1941 and peaked at 427 the following year, with more applications being refused than ever before. Twenty-four students came from war-ravaged Burma and Malay, as did many others whose families had been evacuated from Eastern India.

As the War dragged on, the School continued to do its bit towards the imperial cause by donating the modest funds set aside for

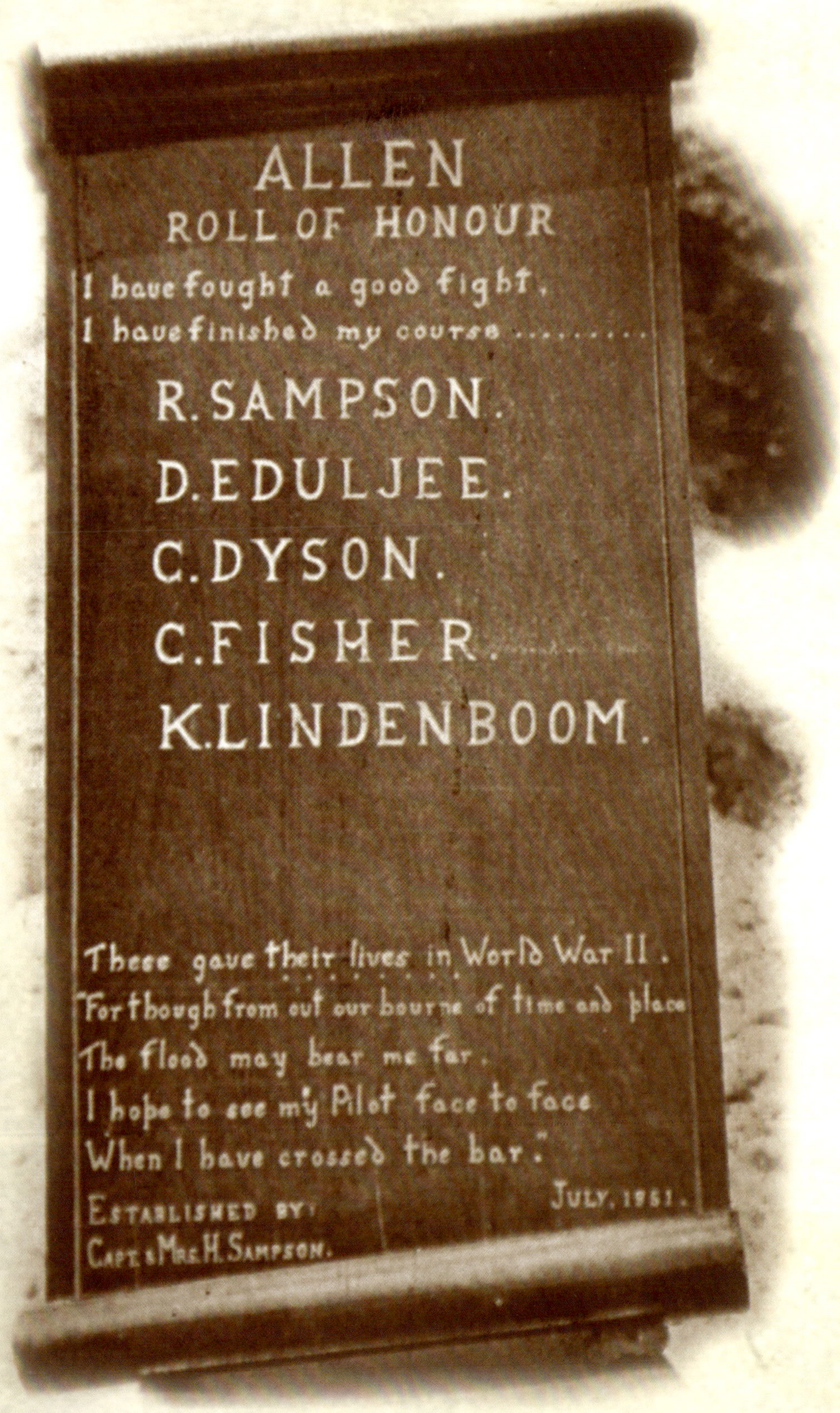

ALLEN
ROLL OF HONOUR

I have fought a good fight,
I have finished my course ....

R. SAMPSON.
D. EDULJEE.
C. DYSON.
C. FISHER.
K. LINDENBOOM.

These gave their lives in World War II.
"For though from out our bourne of time and place
The flood may bear me far.
I hope to see my Pilot face to face
When I have crossed the bar."

July, 1951.

Established by:
Capt. & Mrs. H. Sampson.

Annual Awards and Christmas Treats, collecting funds for the British Red Cross, the widows and orphans of Indian soldiers and sundry other causes, and by 1944 donating blood! It drew happiness and pride from the achievements of its old boys and girls, especially all those who were engaged in the War Effort in some way or the other. News that there were enough old boys in Iraq to have had a successful 'Bala' football match brought cheer, as did the suggestion that an Old Boys Fund be set up to build a swimming pool at Allen.

Top to bottom: Pilot Officer Charles Dyson, Royal Air Force; Charles Joyce Meynell Fisher, who died in the War.

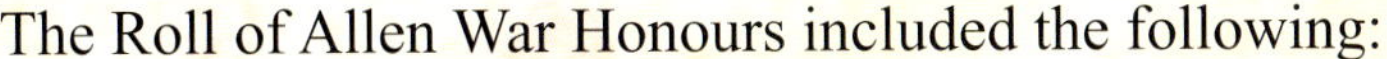

The Roll of Allen War Honours included the following:

- Sqd Ldr Charles Dyson, D.F.C. & Bar, D.S.O. (R.A.F.): Conspicuous bravery in North Africa; holds record for destroying six Capronis in 15 minutes; killed in operations in India.
- Lt Minoo Dinshaw, I.D.S.M. (R.I.N.): Devotion to duty when in charge of Wireless Control in H.I.M.S. Bengal in action with Japanese Raiders.
- Pilot Officer Dinshaw Eduljee, Air Force Cross (R.I.A.F.): Awarded for long and meritorious service in training pilots at Ambala. Killed in operations in Burma.
- Major John Witmarsh-Knight, M.C. (15th Punjab Regiment): Awarded for gallantry at Imphal and Kohima.

The Annual Report for 1941 had been at pains to establish the new profile the Schools had begun to enjoy among the larger public with steadily improving academic performance, availability of better quality teachers and a sea-change in its infrastructural facilities:

> There is still an idea spread far that the Wynberg Homes form an Orphanage of the old style. We glory in the fact that still as in the past no destitute child is refused help and a chance in life, while funds permit. But let it be emphasised strongly — these schools are good schools, taking their place among the best, with boys and girls who are among the best, and going out into life to adorn the avenues they enter with worthy service…no schools of this nature have staffs more highly qualified academically and professionally, and very few as well qualified as ours. None certainly have staffs more wholly dedicated to their calling.

With Rev Biggs as Principal, the 1940s witnessed a period of spectacular flowering — both spiritually and materially. Major and Mrs Lehmann who presided over the closing function of the School year for 1944 were struck by the remarkable changes, Mrs Lehmann being the daughter of the Allen after whom the Boys' School had been named and whose mother had always taken a keen interest in the School's steadily-improving fortunes. With much of the construction activity initiated during the 1930s now being complete, the School sported a spanking new look. Yet for all its visible prosperity, it continued to draw joy from what it regarded as its 'primary purpose', namely to provide a welcoming home for orphan and destitute children. Year after year, the School Board accepted the legal guardianship of orphans and accepted and maintained either entirely free or on very low fees these boys and girls who had nowhere to go; after they completed their schooling, the Board sought suitable employment through the good offices of friends and sympathisers or helped in further training and higher education. In 1942, for instance, the Board accepted as Wards of the Wynberg Society Patricia and Edna Fletcher for whom the Ex-Services Association, Cawnpore Branch, paid Rs. 1,000 per year.

Rev W. J. Biggs.

As the War was drawing to a long, tortuous end, it was becoming evident that the problems of the Anglo-Indian community — kept in abeyance while the more pressing duty towards King and Country was being discharged — would require urgent redress. The School Chairman, A. E. Hart, noted in July 1945:

> We continue to solicit the practical and sympathetic help of the public in the cause of Anglo-Indian education in the future India which is almost certain to present new problems and added difficulties for the community we are here to serve.

The changes in India's social, economic and political life — not to mention its schools and colleges — that were lurking around the corner could no longer be restrained. The end of the War in September 1945 brought both joy and misgivings. The old order had changed and a new one was waiting to take shape. Did it hold promise or pain?

Give to the Winds Thy Fears.
Paul Gerhard

Since the administrative reforms initiated in 1921, education had become a provincial subject under the direct control of a Minister who, in turn reported to the Legislature. In the case of Anglo-Indian education, being deemed a 'Provincial reserved subject', it fell directly under the control of a Member of the Council. To further complicate matters, since the grants-in-aid could only be passed after a vote in the Provincial Legislature, there was no guarantee of sympathetic hearing. As long ago as the Simon Commission in 1927, members of the Anglo-Indian community, led by its ablest defender yet Sir Henry Gidney, had demanded that Anglo-Indian education be made a Central subject so that the unevenness could be ironed out and a uniformity of standards and curriculum be maintained across India. The government pondered its feasibility and as per the recommendations of the Irwin Committee felt that education was better off under provincial purview. However, it did concede the need for uniformity which, it felt, could be ensured with the formation of an Inter-Provincial Board and Provincial Boards of Anglo-Indian Education.[5] At the Third Session of the Round Table Conference, the subject of education again came up and on 6-7 April 1933 a conference on Anglo-Indian and European Education was held in Delhi which was inaugurated by the Viceroy and attended by educationists from other minority communities.

In 1944, the Inter-Provincial Board set up a Commission headed by Bishop Barne of Lahore; called the Barnes Education Commission, it noted the importance given to education by the Anglo-Indian community and the fact that 'the future of the Anglo-Indian community was bound up largely with the existence of Anglo-Indian schools.' Of the 316 primary and secondary schools designated as 'Anglo-Indian', 247 were in the plains and 69 in the hills; of these 180 were boarding schools, 33 orphanages. While overall Government expenditure on education had increased by 29% since 1926-27, expenditure on Anglo-Indian schools had declined; evidently, the burden of education had fallen on the community and — when not partly or wholly subsidised — was shared with the parents. The Barnes Commission also found that the average income of an Anglo-Indian parent was Rs. 150-200 per month. Most of them could not afford higher education and, in any case, pupils from this community 'did not like to continue with a purely literary and academic type of education which was not congenital to their aptitudes'; instead these young people, it found, 'had a natural aptitude for handling tools and machines.'

Amongst the most useful findings of the Barnes Commission was the lack of communication skills in the vernaculars among Anglo-Indian students. Frank Anthony, who had increasingly

[5] This section has been built from a reading of Frank Anthony's book; see Chapter entitled 'In the Educational Vanguard'.

My dear Mummy & Daddy Bala Hissar
I hope you
are well & happy at home. Mussoorie
I received your loving 8/1st/Nov/33
~~(letter)~~ letter Dated 24th of October
Glad to hear that you are very
much better at home.
How are Beatie Alec & Hamish
keeping?
Give my love to Mr & Mrs
Myres.
Give my love to Daddy also

I am sorry to say that I never
came anywhere in the heats
my luck is out this year.
How is my pal Pat keeping
Give my best wishes to
him.
Now I must close with

INDIA POSTAGE
NINE PIES
INDIA
CARD
ADDRESS ONLY

of love & kisses
from your
loving
Son
Nelson

Mrs K E Crawford
56 Hazra Road
Ballygunge
Calcutta

Previous page: Guests enjoying Sports Day. Right: Mike Harrison, School Captain, champion sportsman and star athlete.

begun to play a dominant role in matters pertaining to the Anglo-Indian community and who, in many ways, was a natural heir and successor to the legacy of Sir Henry Gidney, had begun to make a persuasive case for evolving an educational policy that was more in tune with the real needs of the pupils. Commenting on the Barnes Commission, Anthony wrote:

> With the momentous political changes and the avowed policy to introduce the regional languages, increasingly, as the media of instruction in the Universities, Anglo-Indian education, if the present standard of instruction in the Indian languages is continued, will be economically suicidal for the Community. Not only will Anglo-Indians not be able to pursue courses of higher studies but they will be disqualified for employment in the most ordinary appointments.

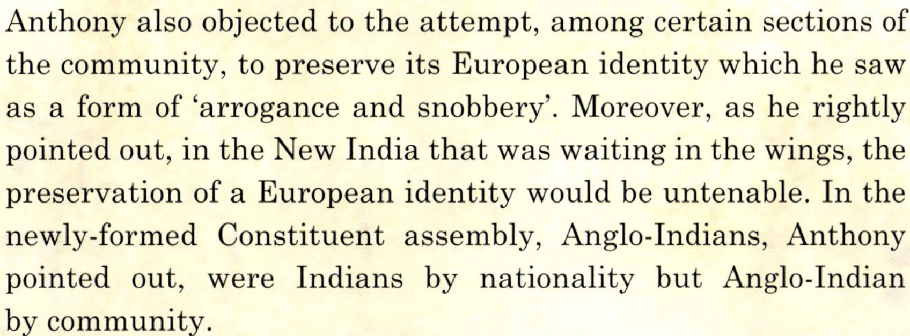

Anthony also objected to the attempt, among certain sections of the community, to preserve its European identity which he saw as a form of 'arrogance and snobbery'. Moreover, as he rightly pointed out, in the New India that was waiting in the wings, the preservation of a European identity would be untenable. In the newly-formed Constituent assembly, Anglo-Indians, Anthony pointed out, were Indians by nationality but Anglo-Indian by community.

Mindful of the ebb and flow of these debates and equally concerned about the future of Anglo-Indian education in India, the members of the Wynberg Society heeded the call of the times. Certain changes were implemented right away: for instance, greater numbers of Indian students were admitted (on full fee), greater emphasis on the teaching of at least one vernacular language (the students being given a choice between Hindi and Urdu in Upper India) began to be given by 1945.[6] Also, for the

[6] A popular call of the time 'No vernacular no employment' was generally understood to be the writing on the wall.

sake of effective internal administration and better coordination as well as more cost-effective running, the School Board decided to reorganise the two Schools — Allen and Wynberg — into one. While separate boarding arrangements would be maintained as would other non-academic work, it was decided that by 1947 classes would be held jointly. This would allow girls to take up Science, if they so wished, and make things more affordable all around at a time when resources were scant and the future signalled a time of even greater uncertainty.

A windfall came by in 1945 with the bequest of Rs. 93,100 from Mr and Mrs G. A. Smith to be utilised in perpetuity as a scholarship for Anglo-Indian children. Along with the Rs. 20,300 already given by them, this money went into the Blanche Hope Smith Scholarship Fund. Mr A. E. Hart who had served the Society as Treasurer for over 40 years retired; before leaving for England, he donated Rs. 10,000 for a scholarship fund. While overall the number of paying students increased, since 40% of the total fee was still being remitted by the Board in the form of partial or full concessions, it was the contribution of generous friends that kept the School out of the red. What was more, War-time financial woes did not end with the War; the steadily worsening political situation pushed up costs of almost all commodities.

The first post-War Annual Report speaks of promise, fear and fulfilment in the year that was 1945. While giving thanks that the War has ended, it notes that there has been no respite from restrictions and anxiety; yet 'the work has been not merely maintained but in some ways enlarged in scope and importance.' The reorganisation of Anglo-Indian education that came in the wake of the various Commissions and their Reports compelled Wynberg Homes to admit 25 extra students. Of the 405 students on roll in 1945, 52% were boys and 26% of Indian birth. Another reorganisational detail noted in the Report is the decision to appoint a separate Headmaster for Allen. The

Principal who had carried the dual responsibility was now free to devote himself solely to administrative and, since the Principal in this case was Rev Biggs, also spiritual matters. Keeping pace with the changing economic climate, the Managing Committee of the Wynberg Society was now rechristened the Board of Governors; the Board members were selected from a wider geographical area and had greater understanding of commercial and industrial matters than before. The year also saw the birth — at Allen — of a remarkable fellowship: the Principals of all ten European high schools at Mussoorie came together to form an Association.[7]

At the close of 1945 — a momentous year by all accounts for the world, the nation and the small community at Wynberg — as the years' gains and losses, hits and misses, successes and failures were being enumerated, the Report closes thus:

> The challenge facing us in India today is that which faced an ancient people entering a new way of life — 'Ye have not been this way heretofore.' It is the challenge that confronted Ruth as she, too, faced national changes — 'Thou art come unto a people which thou knewest not heretofore.' The exhortation of Joshua is ours today — 'Only be thou strong and very courageous.' And Ruth, though she doubtless quailed as she peered ahead, yet clave unto one she trusted and went forward. Perhaps with like fear, but certainly with like trust we must cleave and we do go forward. It is as we do this, with our brethren and our sisters at the crossroads in India, that the promise is to us — "I will not fail thee nor forsake thee. Have I not commanded thee...until the Lord have given your brethren rest.

And with these words of courage and wisdom, Rev Biggs marshalled his flock through the ill tides of Partition. With

[7] I understand that no such Association now exists; evidently, it was dissolved soon after Independence.

FOUNDERS' DAY, 8th October, 1934, 44th Anniversary.

FROM THE SUPERINTENDENT,
PHONE 26.

Wynberg Homes Society

Controlling: The Wynberg Girls' High School. Phone 92.
The Henry Allen Memorial Boys' High School. Phone 212.

Mussoorie, U. P.

MESSAGE TO THE STAFFS.

The Estates of Wynberg, and Bala Hissar, the Home and School Buildings, with hundreds of Girls and Boys uplifted and set upon a pathway to healthy, successful adult life, are unencumbered Monuments to 44 years of progressive benevolent work.

While the Founders, and their Successors, led the building of this great national possession, their words expressed their deep sense of dependence, as humble servants, in the work that became their inspiration and life.

Groups of Experts, of Leaders, by themselves, have never accomplished any enduring economic, or social-economic advancement.

The Leaders of the Wynberg Homes and Schools, from the first, have acknowledged their complete dependence upon God, for His Wisdom and Guidance in their work for the comfort and education of the Children.

With whole-hearted thanks, they have acknowledged the debt of gratitude they owe to many co-builders on all sides: to the honorary workers of the Committee, to every member of the Staffs, a large circle of friends in Mussoorie, the Educational Departments of the U.P., and Government of India, to the Society's Bankers, and to the very many kind and generous people, who comprise the benevolent public of India.

All of these, by their confidence in the Leaders, and with their continuous sympathy, service, advice, and encouraging financial help, are truly co-founders of The Wynberg Homes and Schools. Consequently, all of these friends have a justifiable pride in the living, national possession, unitedly raised high on the Mussoorie Hills, in service to Children of India, and Empire.

In presenting you with this Souvenir Copy of the Proposed Memorial to our late, beloved, Leader, Major F.W. Hart, I sincerely acknowledge and thank you for all you have done to promote the growth of the Homes and Schools, and the welfare of the Children. I am happy to be with you, helping in this great advancing work.

Yours sincerely,

just a few small steps left in the long march to freedom, the country was rocked by communal carnages and the worst acts of bestiality and hatred marring the last years of Imperial rule. At the close of the school year for 1947 in a ceremony presided over by Mrs G. C. P. Allen and Dr Geoffrey Lehmann, the Principal reminded his audience of the horrors of the recent past: burning villages, cries of frightened souls, the school staff defying curfew to bring back loads of washed clothes from the washermen (incidentally all Muslim who I was told by locals had undergone mass conversions to Hinduism only to convert back to Islam after the communal violence had abated somewhat), and the community at Wynberg bravely making do without essentials such as eggs, meat and vegetables and subsisting on beans and marmite and dal cutlets. As the school disbanded for the long winter break, there was no knowing how many would return. Rev Biggs summed up the terrible uncertainty and the immense faith that lay coiled in every heart with the following words:

> The lock of the future is with us; the key is with God; and our glory and trust is in Him.

Partition brought many horrors in its wake, not the least being the gut-wrenching pain of migration. An old student recalls those days thus:

> After Independence in August 1947, many of us at Wynberg-Allen found that our parents and homes were now in Pakistan, a 'foreign' country. India and Pakistan, because of the Hindu-Muslim enmity, were not on friendly terms, to say the least. It did not mean anything to us schoolchildren at the time, but it became a serious problem when we had to cross the border to return home four months later. Rev Biggs along with heads of other schools arranged for us to cross the border together in a convoy of buses, complete with an armed escort. There were some anxious moments for us along the way, which I would not like to experience again.

We shall begin the next chapter with testimonies of some more students who recall those days immediately after Independence as a time of churning and change.

1948-1968

LEARNING
TO ADAPT
The Years of
Trial and Tribulation

Sports Day, 1965 — Mr McNicoll (Junior School Headmaster), Mr C. M. Macmillan and Rev Biggs.

From every mountainside,
let freedom ring.
Samuel F. Smith

While the world slept and India awoke to freedom on the midnight of 15 August 1947, it was amply clear to the community at Wynberg-Allen that it was time for some hard thinking.[1] The Principal's Report for this cataclysmic year gives an indication of the clear-sightedness of those at the helm of affairs: 'We have lost yesterday, unless we learn its lesson. Today is ours but this too we may lose unless we seek to know and to prepare for tomorrow's needs.' At the same time, the Report also gives a glimpse of the doubts and misgivings about a future that was, to say the least, uncertain:

> Does the bridge we are constructing really cross the river, and is it meant to wear, or is it a camouflage largely for attracting attention? Does it really lead in the direction we should be going or does it take us into the wilderness? Is it truly-laid and strong enough to bear the burden the future is already thrusting on it from the other side?

These doubts are important; they show a community that found itself at a crossroads at a crucial juncture in its history. They also show that instead of breaking ranks in disarray, instead of giving

[1] Interestingly enough while Mussoorie — like large swathes of Upper India — was rocked by communal disturbances, riots, arson and looting, at another level life went on as usual for the hedonists who flocked to this hill station. A glance through old copies of The Mussoorie Advertiser for the year 1947 (found in the private collection of Mr Pramode Sawhney, Old Boy of the batch of 1956) carries listings of balls, movies, parties and notices for dinner-dance and cabaret shows as well as charity events. Movies like 'My Darling Clementine' and 'Black Beauty' were running at The Majestic and there seems no portent of the disaster that was playing out in different parts of the country.

in to dismay, it chose to do as thorough a reality check as was possible under the circumstances. Apart from the pressing issue of physical safety and well-being in those turbulent times, education and employment appeared to be two key areas of concern. Already, the ground had been prepared for the use of the term 'Anglo-Indian schools' (instead of the previously-used 'European schools') to denote a system of education with certain attributes free from any 'communal' traits. The Report of the Anglo-Indian Education Commission, discussed in the previous chapter, had made certain recommendations, namely:

(a) Identification with the Indian way of life;

(b Continuance of Anglo-Indian schools and their special character;

(c) Provision of facilities for boys and girls in handicrafts and technical education;

(d) Free and compulsory education for all Anglo-Indian children from the age of six to fourteen; and

(e) Setting up of employment bureaus for Anglo-Indian students and a career master/mistress to assist school leavers to find suitable work.

The staff and Board at Wynberg-Allen found the way forward in these recommendations. They thought it advisable for the children leaving their school to be imbued with a proper appreciation of all that was valuable in the culture of their country so that upon leaving school they could participate fully in all aspects of Indian national life. Renewed importance was, therefore, given to the teaching of Urdu and Hindi; the motto for admission being 'No vernacular, no room!' The School thoroughly approved of the importance given to technical education and for the need of students to move to institutions of higher learning to gain vocational training.

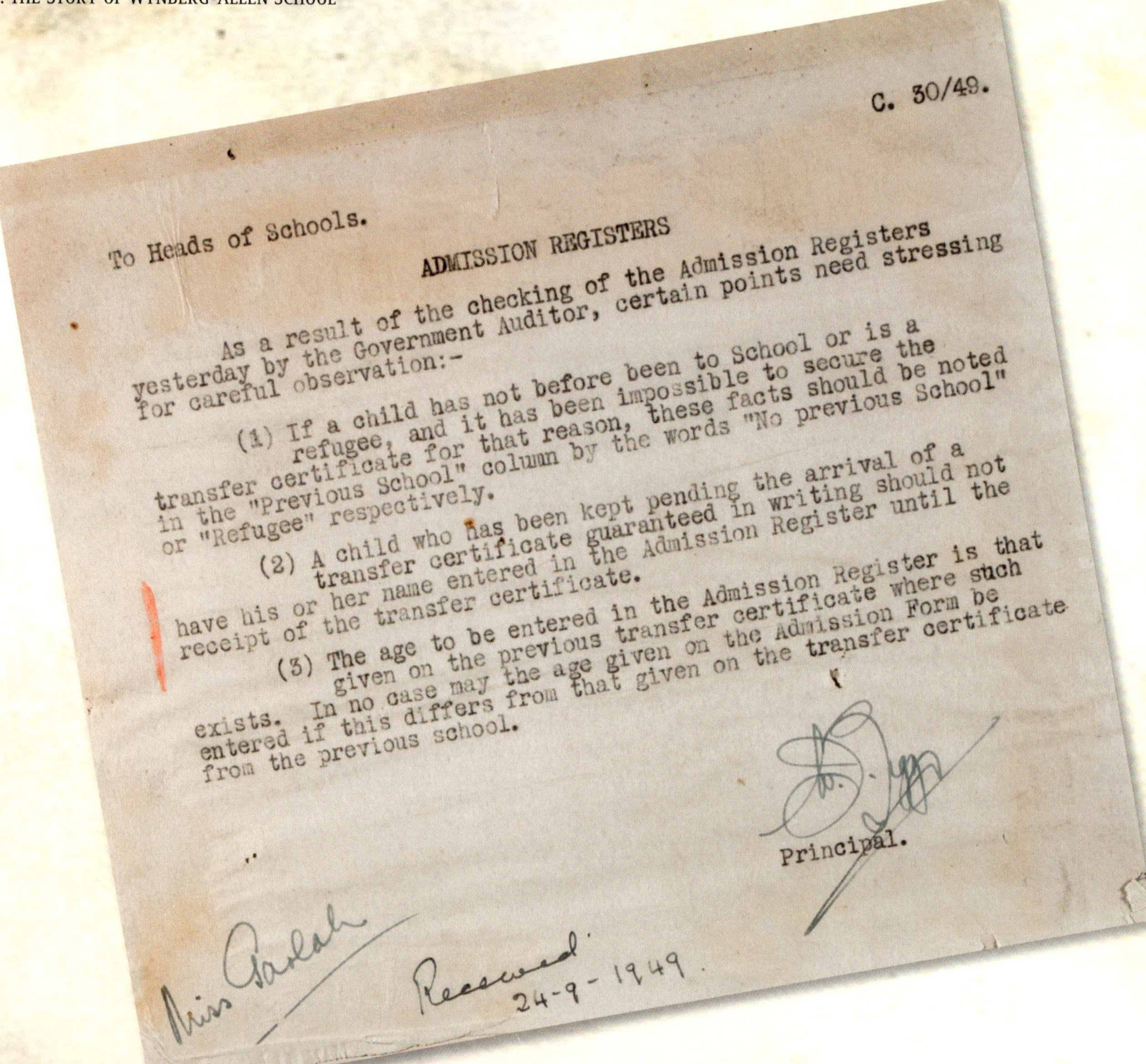

C. 30/49.

To Heads of Schools.

ADMISSION REGISTERS

As a result of the checking of the Admission Registers yesterday by the Government Auditor, certain points need stressing for careful observation:-

(1) If a child has not before been to School or is a refugee, and it has been impossible to secure the transfer certificate for that reason, these facts should be noted in the "Previous School" column by the words "No previous School" or "Refugee" respectively.

(2) A child who has been kept pending the arrival of a transfer certificate guaranteed in writing should not have his or her name entered in the Admission Register until the receipt of the transfer certificate.

(3) The age to be entered in the Admission Register is that given on the previous transfer certificate where such exists. In no case may the age given on the Admission Form be entered if this differs from that given on the transfer certificate from the previous school.

Principal.

Received 24-9-1949.

Several important developments had been taking place on the educational front all through the 1940s. The Anglo-Indian Education Reorganisation Scheme had envisaged the integration of the Anglo-Indian schools into the national stream of education, retaining the finest elements of the past and introducing new principles in keeping with the new message of freedom that was blowing in the wind. Various things needed to be changed with the advent of independence from colonial rule, most notably rules for staff appointments, salaries, promotions, leave, etc. Glaring disparities between the salaries of principals and other staff too needed to be removed. A few months before Independence, in April 1947, the percentage of Indian students permitted in Anglo-Indian schools had been raised from 25 to 40. Under Government orders, seven non-Christian holidays had been added and, in order to make up the annual attendance, certain monthly holidays had been curtailed.

At the end of the first year in Free India, the School took stock. All around, Anglo-Indian hill schools were closing or struggling to keep going under increasing odds.[2] Depleting Government aids, dwindling students, departing staff and faculty added to the dismay that the Anglo-Indian community found itself mired in. Spiralling food prices, unabated communal tensions, galloping inflation, large-scale migration coupled with rampant unemployment and homelessness combined to create an atmosphere of uncertainty and confusion. While many schools buckled under, Wynberg-Allen found unexpected reserves of strength to keep going. No matter how straitened its circumstances, it still had much to be thankful for. A reputation for providing a solid education, a team of dedicated teachers, a deeply-ingrained sense of dignity and pride in the vocation of teaching built over the years were more than enough to stand it in good stead. The presence of Rev Biggs as Principal lent the much-needed gravitas.

[2] Caineville, for instance, a school for girls, closed down and the property was later bought by the Indo-Tibetan Border Police (ITBP).

Wise, compassionate, devoted to the School and its students, Rev Biggs was a visionary. He could look into the future and see the shape of a changing India, a fledgling nation that needed commitment from not one or two sections or communities but from all its citizens in the pressing task of nation-building. He taught his staff and students — by word and deed — how to tighten one's belt and keep moving. He ensured that even in the troubled years immediately after Partition, matches were played, classes were conducted, examinations were cleared and the business of education carried on nonetheless. Addressing his students on Prize Day in November 1947 in the presence of Mrs Allen, who was visiting her beloved school after a hiatus of many years, and her daughter Monica and son-in-law Dr Lehmann who had begun to evince an increasing interest in Wynberg-Allen, Rev Biggs said:

> To stand still is to sit down. India today demands, as she has always needed, schools that understand her longings, that inspire love and longing for her, that fit her children for her life and yet make her worthy of her children. Where in India is a school more devoted to this very aim for sixty years than Wynberg-Allen? Where is there a school more fitted for this very privilege and purpose than ours? And where a Managing Board and Staff more dedicated to that high ideal — the education of India's children for India's life and this the more worthily since we seek that this education shall be in and through the knowledge and power of God?

Some very determined changes were made in the School syllabus. While the emphasis on the teaching of Urdu and Hindi that had begun from the mid-40s was taken up with fresh enthusiasm, even the teaching of history was subjected to a thorough review. Rev Biggs understood that the teaching of 'Empire history' would evoke hostility in some quarters; therefore in his Annual Report for 1948, he was at pains to clarify that:

Peace

The dove, a symbol, nothing more.
The world knows naught of rest.
But like the seas from shore to shore,
In turmoil, tumult, wild uproar,
The waves bring up much dirt and mire
In movements which will never tire
And nothing can arrest.

Peace, peace, this hopeless cry I hear,
But there is never peace.
Like mountains rising in the air,
Which echo back the world's despair.
No, it will never find its quest,
Nor ever will the earth be blest
And find its troubles cease.

Until the Prince of Peace returns
And reigns upon the earth,
And mankind turns to God and yearns
To follow Him and His way learns,
Then only will it find true peace
And ever will its joys increase
For it will know rebirth.

—G.D. Lehmann

13

CHAIRMAN OF WYNBERG-ALLEN SCHOOL FROM 1947-1984.
& SON IN LAW OF MR. HENRY ALLEN

> The history we teach from now must, on the basis of the development of all peoples, be our history — it must be directed to an understanding of India's past and heritage, India's civic life and needs, India's receiving from the world and her giving forth: and it must be related not to one people nor to one empire. It is inevitable that the last two centuries should, with all their vast change, appear but an incidental pocket of time in the vast horizon of India's history; and that period should assume only such importance in our future study.

Myrtle Tindale (nee Hurst), who studied at Wynberg from 1946 till 1952 (Class IV to Senior Cambridge), recalled Rev and Mrs Biggs and their contribution to School life with enormous affection. 'Mama Biggs' and 'Papa Biggs' — as the girls called the Principal and his wife (a lady with a charming lisp whose r's sounded like w's) — showered the students with kindly attention. While Rev Biggs personally escorted some children to their homes across the newly-created border, he taught the ones who stayed behind to protect their Muslim friends. Young though she was at the time of Partition, Myrtle recalled the madness of those tumultuous days, the stories of communal riots and the sudden influx of refugees in Mussoorie. She also had vivid memories of groups of louts who lurked near the playground and how Wynberg girls were tutored to say there were no Muslim students if anyone were to ask and not to call out the names of their Muslim peers while playing on the flats or going into town.[3]

Myrtle's sister Dagma Houghton (nee Hurst) spoke of the value-based education of her time. Though poor as Church mice, compared for instance to the 'Woodstock girls' whom the Wynberg girls both admired and envied, they nevertheless had ample fun

---

[3] Hugh Gantzer, who joined Hampton Court in 1939, well remembers the madness of the Partition years. He was studying at St George's as the time for Partition drew near and recalls the name tags of Muslim boys being changed to safeguard them. Hugh's father, who retired as Director of Surveys, Bihar and Orissa, and was also Chairman of the City Board, Mussoorie, protected their Muslim neighbours Hamid and Sharifa Ali during the riots that scarred Mussoorie.

Facing page: Children participating in games, 1965.

at School. The Hurst sisters recall receiving 4 annas[4] as pocket money every Saturday which would be spent on 'jigs and jags' (peanuts and jaggery); or a tin of condensed milk (pierced with two holes, it was a treat to suck its sweet contents); or buying a pack of 'K-Rations' (comprising cheese, biscuits, fruit bar and Camel cigarettes, it would be smuggled from American depots and sold in black in the town); or buying romantic novels (the most popular being *Forever Amber,* set during the reign of Charles II, it was a huge hit with teenage girls as was *Gone with the Wind*). Once a month, they would be treated to a movie that cost 8 annas. Often, when the girls couldn't pay, the teachers pitched in.[5] Sometimes, when they had exhausted their weekly pocket money, the girls would eat sorrel that grew wild on the hills or wild raspberries that they called 'Achoos', or even Fox's Grapes, a dark blue berry that grew abundantly among the bushes; if caught eating such inappropriate things by their teachers, they would promptly be given a dose of castor oil! School food, back then, was notoriously bad: watery dal for breakfast, boiled eggs once a week and powdered egg omelette on Sundays; a rare treat would be pork once a week. And an annual treat would be the Founders' Day Dinner comprising pulau, mutton curry and huge jalebis which they called jalebas!

[4] Pramode Sawhney told me that the School slang for 4 annas was 'charzee'; a 'charzee' could also buy you a chunk of 'stick jaw' from the Tuck Shop.

[5] Both Myrtle and Dagma felt that their teachers were incredibly committed. Possibly because many were spinsters, they devoted themselves wholeheartedly to their young wards. Also, the Christian spirit of charity was stronger among the teaching community back then, they feel. For instance, two spinsters, Eva and May Beans took in orphans during the long winter holidays. The Hurst sisters recall the Anglo-Indian children from Calcutta being richer and smarter, especially those whose parents worked for the Customs or the Railways. Also, while the richer kids bought foreign pretzels, condensed milk and tinned goodies, the others brought back 'tuck' comprising home-made pickles, jams and biscuits. By and large, the girls at Wynberg were as puritan and prudish as their teachers. Segregation was always strict between the boys and the girls and perhaps the naughtiest thing they ever did was to tie bed-sheets to escape from their dorms and run into town to buy 'puri tack' (tarkari)! Myrtle also remembered the night toilet being a favourite hangout for night-time reading and the shout-out call of 'Chivs' or 'KV' (probably cavee, from the Latin cave meaning to keep a look out) to alert those up to some mischief. Dagma recalls seeing Sikhs for the first time after Partition when two Sikh girls were enrolled in their school. She also remembers the Hindi film actor, Bina Rai (whose real name was Krishna Sarin and whose family lived close to the School), studying with her till Class VII till she moved to Lucknow. Myrtle recalled how many girls dreamt of going to study at IT College in Lucknow. Being the Head Girl, Myrtle cut the Founders' Day Cake for the year 1951. Having topped in the Senior Cambridge in her School and stood Third in U.P. in 1952, Myrtle too wanted to go to IT to train to be a teacher. However, financial constraints compelled her to go back home to Saharanpur, learn shorthand-typing and eventually join the ITC where she worked till her retirement. Myrtle passed away on 12 May 2013, during the making of this book.

Enjoying the games, 1965.

The School celebrated its Diamond Jubilee in 1949. Inspired by the words of Apostle Paul, which had for many years now been the School Motto, the School forged on:

> Forgetting those things which are behind and reaching forth
> For those things which are before,
> We press on — Excelsior!

While other schools were crippled or enfeebled by debilitating cuts and denuded classrooms, Wynberg-Allen marched on. What kept it going? What distinguished it from others? To quote Rev Biggs, it was 'the spirit of Wynberg-Allen', an indescribable quality that

bound men and women, young and old into 'a fine fellowship of service'. One outstanding member of this fellowship was Beryl Grace Harding who had come to teach at Wynberg in 1932. After a stint as a war-time nurse, she returned to teach and inspire young lives as a symbol of 'unfailing purpose combined with the tenderest loyalties of friendship'. Upon her passing away, her sister Elsie put up a small memorial in November 1949: a shield embossed with smaller shields, each inscribed with the name of a girl whose conduct has been 'above reproach, particularly in purity of thought and word.[6]

The Beryl Harding Shield.

We are perplexed, yet not unto despair.

2 Corinthians 4:8

The question of religion and religious instruction proved to be a thorny one in the new, secular India that was being forged. The Sargent Scheme,[7] which formed the bedrock of school education till now, had agreed that religion — in the widest sense — should inspire all education and an education devoid of an ethical content would be sterile and barren. The Wynberg Society that had all along been at pains to ensure that an atmosphere of 'the sense of God's grace' permeates the School found itself in a quandary. Would the teaching of Scripture, evangelism, daily worship, weekly Church, etc. stop under the new dispensation? Would the very basis of their existence — a belief in the Kingdom of God — for six decades be taken away? Or, would constitutional safeguards allow sanity to prevail after the frenzy of communal hatred had subsided? How would India, a mint-fresh socialist, secular republic interpret secularism?

[6] Dagma Houghton (nee Hurst who studied at Wynberg from 1942-48) remembers Elsie and Beryl Harding as great teachers, who taught her when she was in Standard V. Myrtle Hurst received the Beryl Harding Shield in 1951.

[7] Sir John Sargent, the Educational Adviser to the Government of India was asked to prepare a comprehensive report on education. His report, also called the Sargent Scheme, was submitted to the Central Advisory Board of Education (CABE) in 1944.

Again, the wisdom and perspicacity of Rev Biggs rose to the occasion. In his Annual Day speech for 1949, he declared: 'I do not apologise for giving first consideration to the spiritual.' Moreover, the Constitution of India, which was being drafted by men like Dr B. R. Ambedkar, had due regard for the minorities; thanks to men like Frank Anthony, healthy checks and balances were being

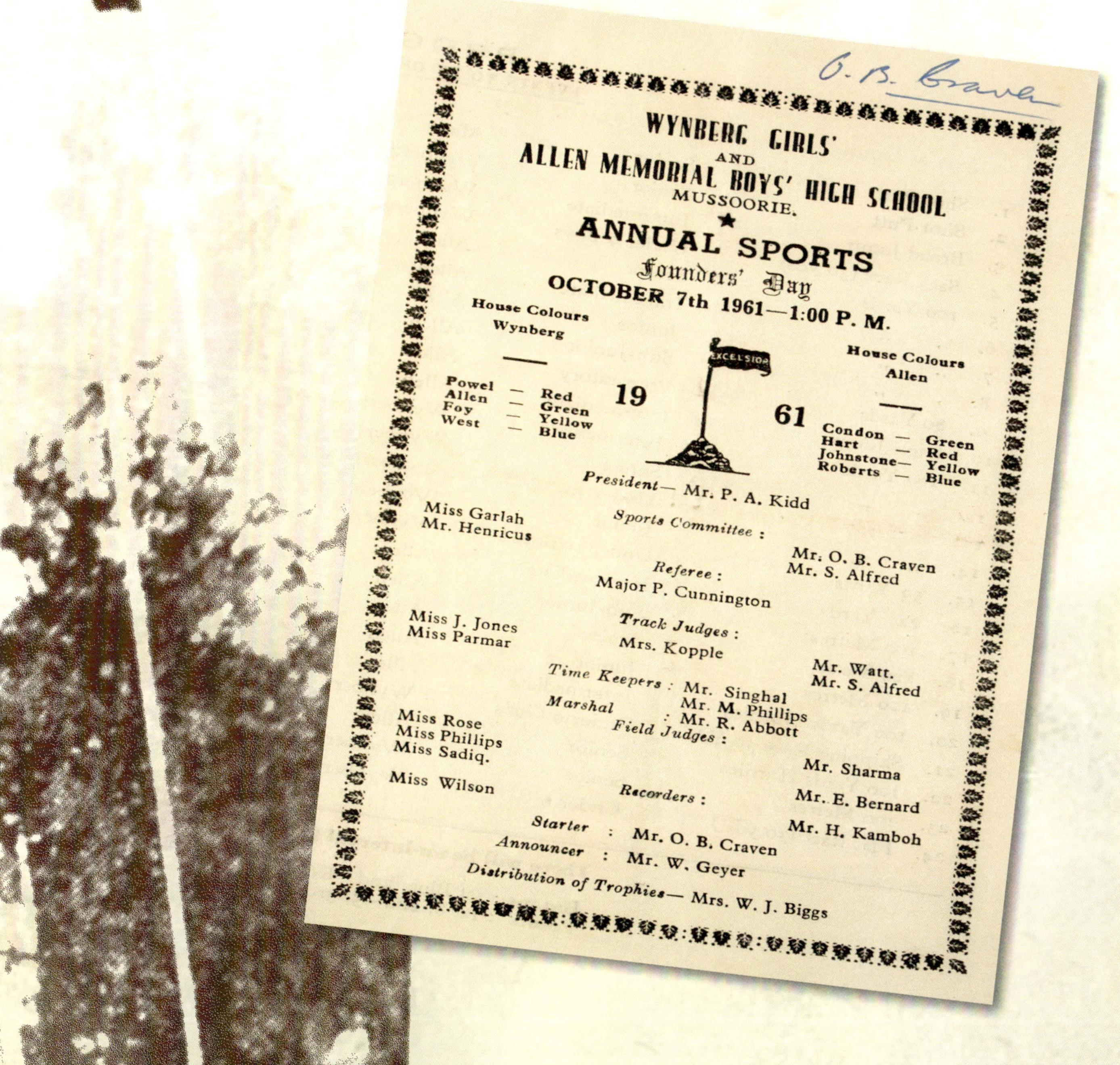

O. B. Craven

WYNBERG GIRLS'
AND
ALLEN MEMORIAL BOYS' HIGH SCHOOL
MUSSOORIE.
★
ANNUAL SPORTS
Founders' Day
OCTOBER 7th 1961—1:00 P. M.

House Colours
Wynberg

Powel — Red
Allen — Green
Foy — Yellow
West — Blue

19 EXCELSIOR 61

House Colours
Allen

Condon — Green
Hart — Red
Johnstone— Yellow
Roberts — Blue

President— Mr. P. A. Kidd

Sports Committee :
Miss Garlah
Mr. Henricus
Mr. O. B. Craven
Mr. S. Alfred

Referee :
Major P. Cunnington

Track Judges :
Miss J. Jones
Miss Parmar
Mrs. Kopple
Mr. Watt.
Mr. S. Alfred

Time Keepers : Mr. Singhal
Mr. M. Phillips
Marshal : Mr. R. Abbott

Field Judges :
Miss Rose
Miss Phillips
Miss Sadiq.
Mr. Sharma

Recorders :
Miss Wilson
Mr. E. Bernard
Mr. H. Kamboh

Starter : Mr. O. B. Craven
Announcer : Mr. W. Geyer
Distribution of Trophies— Mrs. W. J. Biggs

put in place which would allow India's pluralistic, multi-cultural, multi-ethnic, multi-lingual population the right to also practise its faith without fear or favour. Rev Biggs was unequivocal in his assertion:

> We MUST find our mainspring, our purpose and our strength in the spiritual. For those of us who are Christian we must cherish our privilege of worship, we must seek and know the will of God through a study and love of the Bible, and we must with sincerity and devotion make clear through the witness of work and life that faith that is ours and the debt we owe to our Lord.

MUSSOORIE SCHOOLS' SPORTS ASSOCIATION.

INTER SCHOOL

BOXING

5:00 P. M. ON

August 20th, 21st, & 22nd.
(1958)

OFFICIALS

By kind permission of

The Commandant, 58 GORKHA TRAINING CENTRE, DEHRA DUN,

AND

The Commandant, Military College, DEHRA DUN,

The following will officiate.

REFEREE:—MAJOR M. S KINNER.

JUDGES ; Capt.—S. NORTON.
Capt.—S. N. BILIMORIA.
Capt.—H C. ATTRI.

TIME KEEPER:—M. J. DEY.

M. C.:—Mr. A. F. REGHELINI,

M. O.:—Dr. J. K. DATTA.

Art Press Mussoorie

The post-1947 years saw a sharp drop in numbers. By 1949, the School had lost 102 students; a great many had gone overseas, some could not return from Pakistan, still others chose to go to schools nearer home rather than risk the long journey to and fro in those uncertain times. But the School remained undeterred, knowing fully well that numbers spell finances. While it had opened its doors to Hindus, Muslims, Sikhs, Parsis as well as native Christian children, its concern remained with the needy Anglo-Indian child. A sister society, the Wynberg Homes Society of Great Britain, was set up in 1949 to help with financial transfusions. Rev and Mrs Biggs took a year's furlough and toured Britain in 1950, met friends such as Mrs Allen, the Lehmanns, the Perry family, as well as scattered old boys and girls. Everyone agreed: there was a need — more than ever before — for every man and woman to rise to the occasion and come to the help of the Wynberg

Homes. Help — both financial and moral — came from individuals and institutions in India and abroad, such as: the Bengal Masonic Association, the Delhi Ex-Services Association, the Lahore and Delhi Diocesan Boards, the Dehra Dun Women's Benevolent Society, the European Schools Improvement Association (U.P. Branch), Bible Presbyterian Mission in Kanpur, the British India Corporation Limited, among many who preferred to remain nameless.

Meanwhile, despite mounting pressure from the State Education Department to reconstitute managing committees of even recognised registered societies such as that of Wynberg Homes, the Board of Management resolutely remained in Christian hands. The School took heed of the words from the Bible:

> Enlarge the place of thy tent: lengthen thy cords: strengthen thy stakes. (Isaiah. 54.2)

The School interpreted it thus: 'ensure stability at the time of the storm but prepare for growing opportunities that the Lord will send you.' And, indeed the Lord kept sending many opportunities. Gradually the School managed to restore its nominal rolls as a steady influx of students kept pouring in: from Ceylon, Burma and

PREVIOUS RECORDS

	Event	Record	Holder
Under	10 Broad Jump	13 ft. 1½ ins.	P. Jervis, St. George's 1944
"	10 Cricket Ball Throw	161ft. 3 ins.	P. Davidson St Fidels' 1943
"	10 60 yards Dash	8.3 Secs	R. Francis, Allen MemorialSch 1948
"	10 440 yards Relay	63.4 Secs.	Oak Grove, 1942
"	12 Cricket Ball throw	200 ft.	Aminuddin, Doon School 1939
"	12 Brod Jump	14 ft. 8¾ ins.	P. Castellino, St, George's 1942
"	12 80 yards Dash	10.0 secs	C. Beecham, Allen Memorial 1948
"	12 440 yards Relay	59.2 secs	St. George's 1942
"	14 100 yards Dash	11.6 secs	M. O'Brien, St. George's 1945
"	14 220 yards Dash	26.8 secs	M. O'Brien, St George's, 1945
"	14 Broad Jump	16ft. 11 ins	S. Mraherd St. George's 1953 & M. Hookens Allen 1955
"			
"	14 High Jump	4 ft. 11¾ ins.	L. Rockey, Woodstock 1943
"	14 Pole Vault	8 ft. 6 ins.	B. Recontre Woodstock 1942
"	14 440 yards Relay	55.2 secs	Oak Grove 1943
"	16 100 yards Dash	10.6 secs	C. Norris, St. George's 1945
"	16 220 yards Dash	24.8 secs	B. Staynor, Oak Grove, 1944
"	16 880 yards	2 mins 18.8sec	S. Bahaguna, Allen Memorial, 1950
"	16 High Jump	5ft. 5½ ins.	D. Williamson, Oak Grove, 1943
"	16 Pole Vault.	9ft. 9 ins.	E. Lys, St. George's 1941
"	16 Hop. step & Jump	39 ft. 6 ins.	A. Dale. St George's 1941
"	16 Shot Putt	40 ft. 1 in.	A. Dale, St. George's 1942
"	16 880 yards Relay	1min 40.8sec	Oak Grove, 1944
"	18 100 yards Dash	10.4 sces	L. Smith, St. George's 1942
"	18 220 yards	24.5 secs	D. Hollingberry, Woodstock, 1942
"	18 440 yards	53.4 secs	G. Howard, Woodstock, 1942
"	18 880 yards Relay	1 min 41 secs	Oak Grove, 1942
"	18 High Jump	5ft. 7 ins.	G. Howard, Woodstock 1942
"	18 Shot Putt	45 ft 5½ ins.	H. McMillan, Woodstock 1942
"	18 Pole Vault	10ft 8 ins	D. Mylne S.G.C., 1952
"	18 Broad Jump	19ft 10 ins	D. Graham Woodstock 1943
"	Hop. Step & Jump	43 ft 3½ in	D. Mylne S. G. C, 1952
"	18 880 yards	2 mins 13sec	D. Skinner St. George's 1947
"	Discus	104 ft. 0 ins	K. Dye Woodstock 1950
"	Javelin	139 ft. 7½ins	B Duke, S. G. C, 1955
"	Hurdles	13 5 secs	P Corbett. O. G. 1955.
Open	100 yards Dash	10.4 secs	D. Wide. St. Fidelis 1938.
"	440 yards	55.4 secs	D. Kelleher St George's 1940
"	Discus	109 ft 11ns.	L. McCulloch Woodstock 1944
"	Javelin	149 ft 7 ins	P. Alexander Oak Grove 1952
"	100 yards Hurdles	13.2 sec	I. Alexander Oak Grove 1953
"	One mile	4min 59.4sec	V. Barretto. St. George's 1954

Two championships are awaarded .. ....Junior and Senior.
The School scoring the greatest number of points in :
Under 10, Under12, Under14 is declared the winner of the Junior Championshisp
The school scoring the greatest number of points in :
Under 16 and Under 18 is declared winner of the Senior Championship:
For the purpose of determining the Championship. points 4, 3, 2 and 1 in each of the five divisions for 1st 2nd. 3rd. & 4th are counted, instead of the aggregate number of points. (In the event of tie: in either Division, aggregate points will determine the Championship)
Points awarded are 5, 3, 2 and 1 for 1st, 2nd, 3rd, and 4th., respectively. For relays the points are 8,5,3,2, and 1.

Africa as well as different parts of independent India. Children of landed aristocracy, bureaucrats, businessmen, military men, as well as needy Anglo-Indian families kept coming in sufficiently large numbers. As the Report for 1952 put it: 'Our sphere is Anglo-Indian education, but our vision is India, our purpose India's life in God through us.'

By 1950, the first company of the National Cadet Corps (NCC) in Anglo-Indian schools in Mussoorie had been inaugurated. With a characteristic 'never-say-die' spirit, Allen transferred the efficiency and smartness it had demonstrated in its A.F. Detachment of former years to the new NCC wing. The School

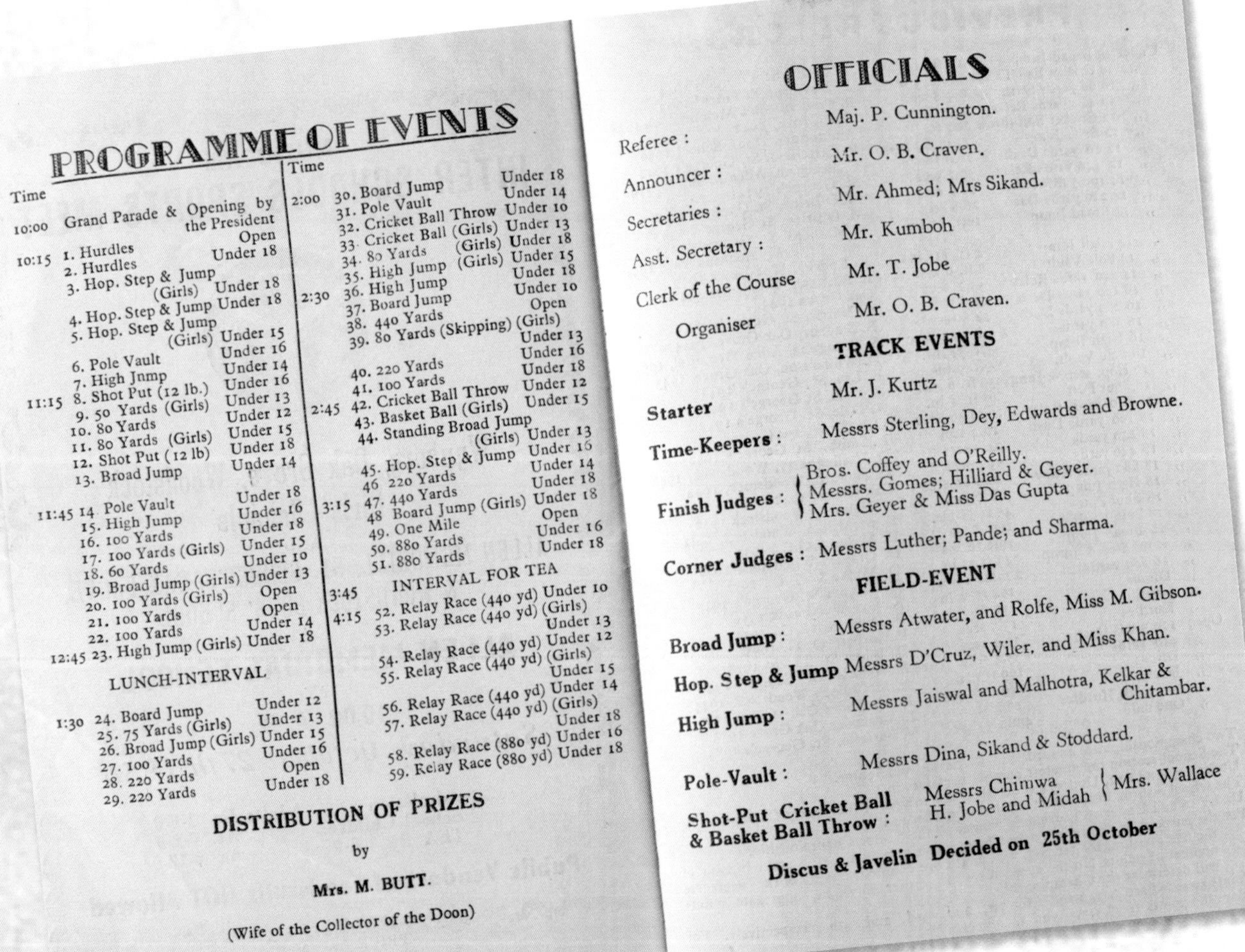

PROGRAMME OF EVENTS

Time
10:00 Grand Parade & Opening by the President
Open
10:15 1. Hurdles Under 18
2. Hurdles
3. Hop. Step & Jump (Girls) Under 18
4. Hop. Step & Jump Under 18
5. Hop. Step & Jump (Girls) Under 15
Under 16
6. Pole Vault Under 14
7. High Jnmp Under 16
11:15 8. Shot Put (12 lb.) Under 13
9. 50 Yards (Girls) Under 12
10. 80 Yards Under 15
11. 80 Yards (Girls) Under 18
12. Shot Put (12 lb) Under 14
13. Broad Jump

Under 18
11:45 14 Pole Vault Under 16
15. High Jump Under 18
16. 100 Yards Under 15
17. 100 Yards (Girls) Under 10
18. 60 Yards Under 13
19. Broad Jump (Girls) Open
20. 100 Yards (Girls) Open
21. 100 Yards Under 14
22. 100 Yards Under 18
12:45 23. High Jump (Girls)

LUNCH-INTERVAL

Under 12
1:30 24. Board Jump Under 13
25. 75 Yards (Girls) Under 15
26. Broad Jump (Girls) Under 16
27. 100 Yards Open
28. 220 Yards Under 18
29. 220 Yards

Time
Under 18
2:00 30. Board Jump Under 14
31. Pole Vault Under 10
32. Cricket Ball Throw Under 13
33. Cricket Ball (Girls) Under 18
34. 80 Yards (Girls) Under 15
35. High Jump (Girls) Under 18
2:30 36. High Jump Under 10
37. Board Jump Open
38. 440 Yards (Girls)
39. 80 Yards (Skipping) Under 13
Under 16
40. 220 Yards Under 18
41. 100 Yards Under 12
2:45 42. Cricket Ball Throw Under 15
43. Basket Ball (Girls)
44. Standing Broad Jump (Girls) Under 13
Under 16
45. Hop. Step & Jump Under 14
46 220 Yards Under 18
3:15 47. 440 Yards Under 18
48 Board Jump (Girls) Open
49. One Mile Under 16
50. 880 Yards Under 18
51. 880 Yards

3:45 INTERVAL FOR TEA
4:15 52. Relay Race (440 yd) Under 10
53. Relay Race (440 yd) (Girls) Under 13
54. Relay Race (440 yd) Under 12
55. Relay Race (440 yd) (Girls) Under 15
56. Relay Race (440 yd) Under 14
57. Relay Race (440 yd) (Girls) Under 18
58. Relay Race (880 yd) Under 16
59. Relay Race (880 yd) Under 18

DISTRIBUTION OF PRIZES

by

Mrs. M. BUTT.

(Wife of the Collector of the Doon)

OFFICIALS

Referee : Maj. P. Cunnington.
Announcer : Mr. O. B. Craven.
Secretaries : Mr. Ahmed; Mrs Sikand.
Asst. Secretary : Mr. Kumboh
Clerk of the Course : Mr. T. Jobe
Organiser : Mr. O. B. Craven.

TRACK EVENTS

Starter : Mr. J. Kurtz
Time-Keepers : Messrs Sterling, Dey, Edwards and Browne.
Finish Judges : Bros. Coffey and O'Reilly. Messrs. Gomes; Hilliard & Geyer. Mrs. Geyer & Miss Das Gupta
Corner Judges : Messrs Luther; Pande; and Sharma.

FIELD-EVENT

Broad Jump : Messrs Atwater, and Rolfe, Miss M. Gibson.
Hop. Step & Jump Messrs D'Cruz, Wiler, and Miss Khan.
High Jump : Messrs Jaiswal and Malhotra, Kelkar & Chitambar.
Pole-Vault : Messrs Dina, Sikand & Stoddard.
Shot-Put Cricket Ball & Basket Ball Throw : Messrs Chimwa H. Jobe and Midah { Mrs. Wallace

Discus & Javelin Decided on 25th October

PROGRAMME

EVENTS TO BE DECIDED ON SPORTS DAY

No.	Event	Class	House
1.	Shot Putt	Senior	Allen
2.	Shot Putt	Senior	Wynberg.
3.	Broad Jump	Intermediate	Wynberg
4.	Sack Race (30 yds)	Under 9 Boys	Wynberg.
5.	100 Yards	Senior	Allen
6.	" "	Intermediate	Allen
7.	" "	Junior	Allen
8.	" "	Sub-Junior	Allen
9.	80 Yards	Preparatory	Allen
10.	High Jump	Intermediate	Allen
11.	100 Yards	Intermediate	Wynberg
12.	" "	Senior	Wynberg
13.	80 Yards	Under 11	Wynberg.
14.	" "	Junior	Wynberg
15.	50 Yards	Under 10 Boys & Girls	Wynberg
16.	220 Yards	Intermediate	Allen
17.	100 Metres	Sub-Junior	Allen
18.	220 Yards	Senior	Allen
19.	100 Metres	Junior	Allen
20.	100 Yards Hurdles	Intermediate	Allen
21.	Skipping Race 50 Yds.	Under 9 Girls	Wynberg.
22.	100 Yards Hurdles	Senior	Allen
23.	100 Metres	Senior	Wynberg
24.	Flat Race (30 yds.)	Under 6	Wynberg.
25.	100 Metres	Intermediate	Wynberg
26.	440 Yards	Senior	Allen
27.	" "	Intermediate	Allen
28.			
29.	50 Yards Skipping	Under 10	Wynberg
30.	30 Yards	Under 7	Wynberg
31.	Skipping Race (80 Yds)	Junior	Wynberg.
32.	House Relay (440 Yds)	Under 10	Wynberg & Allen
33.	880 Yards	Senior	Allen
34.	" "	Intermediate	Allen

TEA INTERVAL

No.	Event	Class	House
35.	March Past Houses		Wynberg & Allen
36.	House Relay (440 yds)	Intermediate	Wynberg
37.	" " " "	Junior	Allen
38.	" " " "	Sub-Junior	Allen
39.	House Relay (880 yds)	Intermediate	Allen
40.	House Relay (440 yds)	Junior	Wynberg
41.	House Relay (880 yds)	Senior	Allen
42.	Servants' Race		
43.	Staff, Old Boys, School Relay		

DISTRIBUTION OF TROPHIES

There will be an Interval for TEA from 3-30 to 4-00 P. M.

Batons : 1st Blue; 2nd - Red; 3rd - Green 4th - Yellow.
Points : 1st 8; 2nd - 5; 3rd - 3; 4th - 2 (Relays-double points).

neither concealed nor flaunted its 'Anglo-Indian evangelism'; it simply carried on, putting up a cheerful front and doing what it knew best: educating young minds. Though, as more and more of the old teachers either departed for their Home in the skies or Back Home to the Old Country or found New Homes in the Commonwealth, the problem of finding experienced staff from among the native Christian community proved to be a vexing one. The ideal solution appeared to be finding committed teachers overseas who would be willing to come over for a worthy cause.

The School also took heart from Article 28 of the newly-drafted Constitution of India. A circular, sent by the Department of Education, brought good cheer to those who saw no need for subterfuge when it came to declaring the Christian

Wynberg, circa 1960s.

bedrock of their institution. The Government circular stated in unequivocal words:

> No religious instruction shall be provided in any Educational institution wholly maintained out of State funds, but nothing... shall apply to *an educational institution which is administered* by the State but has been *established under any endowment or trust which requires that religious instruction shall be imparted* in such institution. No person attending any educational institution receiving aid out of State funds shall

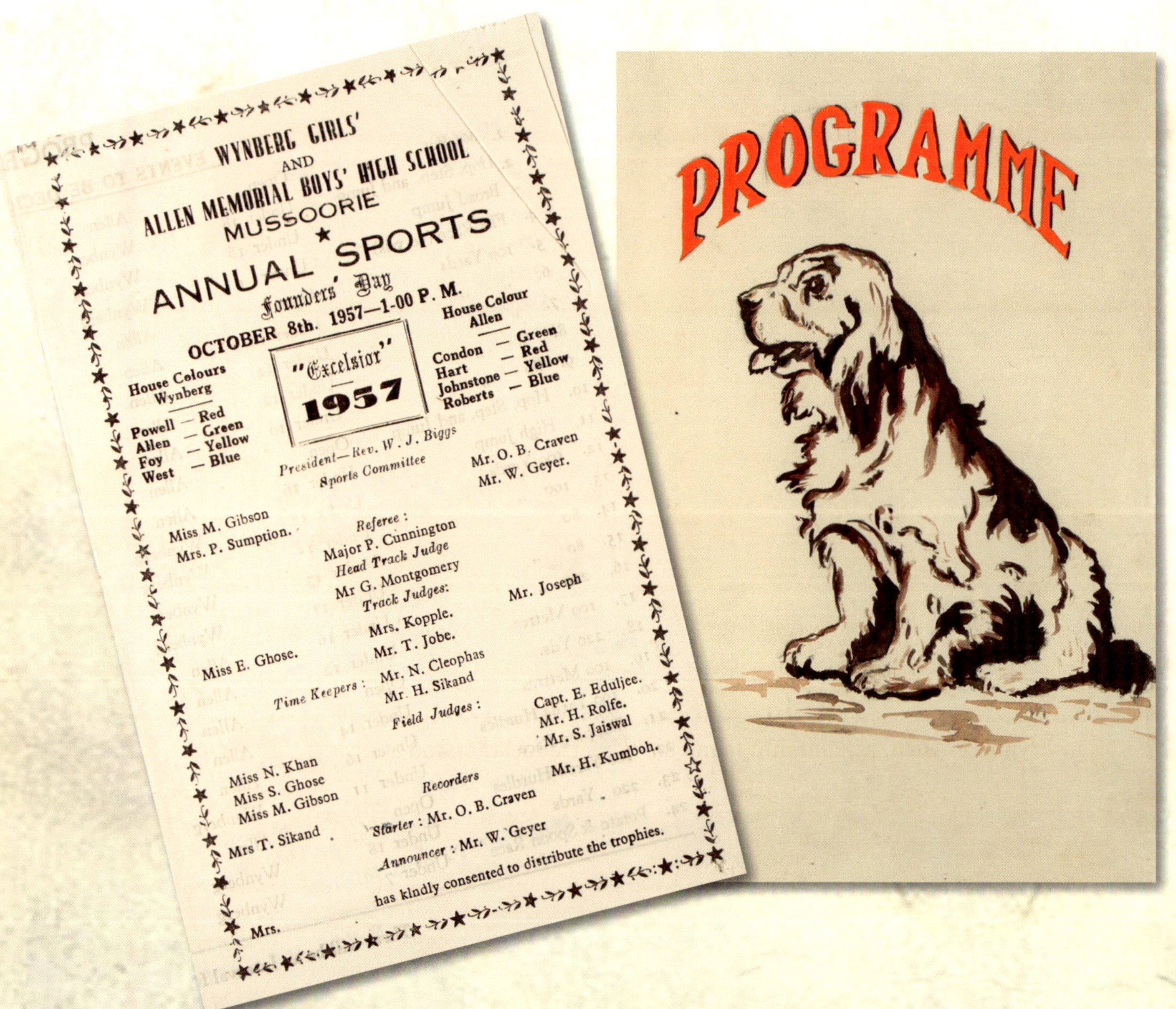

WYNBERG GIRLS'
AND
ALLEN MEMORIAL BOYS' HIGH SCHOOL
MUSSOORIE
★
ANNUAL SPORTS
Founders' Day
OCTOBER 8th. 1957—1-00 P. M.

House Colours Wynberg		"Excelsior" 1957	House Colour Allen	
Powell	— Red		Condon	— Green
Allen	— Green		Hart	— Red
Foy	— Yellow		Johnstone	— Yellow
West	— Blue		Roberts	— Blue

President—Rev. W. J. Biggs

Sports Committee

Miss M. Gibson
Mrs. P. Sumption.
Mr. O. B. Craven
Mr. W. Geyer.

Referee :
Major P. Cunnington

Head Track Judge
Mr G. Montgomery

Track Judges:
Miss E. Ghose.
Mrs. Kopple.
Mr. T. Jobe.
Mr. Joseph

Time Keepers :
Mr. N. Cleophas
Mr. H. Sikand

Field Judges :
Miss N. Khan
Miss S. Ghose
Miss M. Gibson
Capt. E. Edulje.
Mr. H. Rolfe.
Mr. S. Jaiswal

Recorders
Mrs T. Sikand
Mr. H. Kumboh.

Starter : Mr. O. B. Craven

Announcer : Mr. W. Geyer

Mrs.
has kindly consented to distribute the trophies.

> be required to take part in any religious instruction...to attend any religious worship that may be conducted in such institution... *unless such person is a minor and his guardian has given his consent there-to.*

To this day Wynberg-Allen does not enforce its evangelism; it insists on written permission from the guardians of those non-Christian children who wish, voluntarily, to attend worship.

That there was truth in the adage 'Change is the only Constant' and that the School was learning to adapt to the changing political and social scenario, is amply evident in the Report for 1953-54:

> Now that we have accommodated ourselves and our working to life and conditions which only a few years ago were revolutionary, and our vision of a future that is already with us, it seems we may in the Report turn from a recital of the doings of the Schools and share a little more deeply a knowledge of the situation in which the Society is working today and of the way in which your Board is seeking to fulfil its continuing yet changing trust.

From 1955 onwards, the cuts in educational grants for Anglo-Indian educational institutions that had so far been kept in abeyance came into effect. By 1959 all special considerations granted to Anglo-Indian schools were abolished all together. The School prepared for these eventualities well in advance: income from existing securities (such as the Blanche Hope Smith Scholarship Fund) was used to train the School's own graduating students to become teachers in their own School and in the process not merely help the School Society and the Anglo-Indian community but also add to the self-sufficiency of the community. A sum of Rs. 6,000 was set aside in 1952 to be used as foundationer-ships in Wynberg-Allen, scholarship loans for higher education and grants for teacher training. Funds collected by friends overseas mitigated, somewhat, the anxiety of delayed government grants and expensive bank overdrafts.

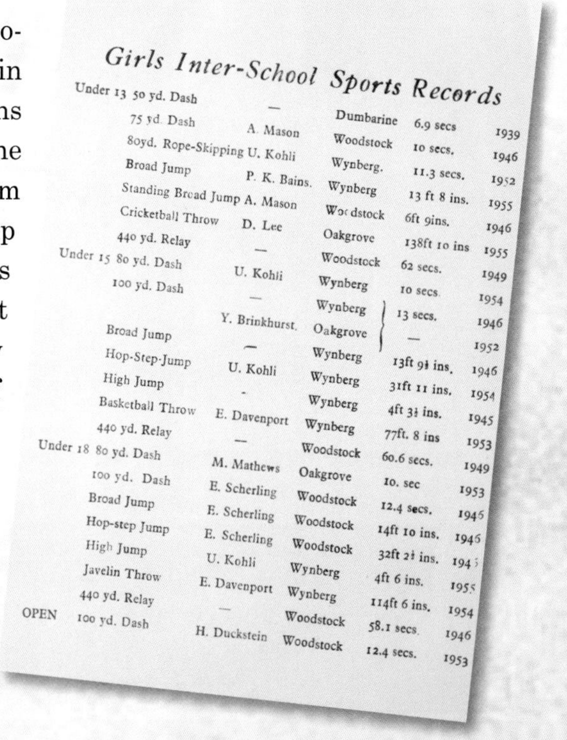

Girls Inter-School Sports Records

Under 13	50 yd. Dash	—	Dumbarine	6.9 secs	1939
	75 yd. Dash	A. Mason	Woodstock	10 secs.	1946
	80yd. Rope-Skipping	U. Kohli	Wynberg.	11.3 secs.	1952
	Broad Jump	P. K. Bains.	Wynberg	13 ft 8 ins.	1955
	Standing Broad Jump	A. Mason	Woodstock	6ft 9ins.	1946
	Cricketball Throw	D. Lee	Oakgrove	138ft 10 ins	1955
	440 yd. Relay	—	Woodstock	62 secs.	1949
Under 15	80 yd. Dash	U. Kohli	Wynberg	10 secs.	1954
	100 yd. Dash	—	Wynberg	13 secs.	1946
		Y. Brinkhurst.	Oakgrove	—	1952
	Broad Jump	—	Wynberg	13ft 9½ ins.	1946
	Hop-Step-Jump	U. Kohli	Wynberg	31ft 11 ins.	1954
	High Jump	-	Wynberg	4ft 3½ ins.	1945
	Basketball Throw	E. Davenport	Wynberg	77ft. 8 ins	1953
	440 yd. Relay	—	Woodstock	60.6 secs.	1949
Under 18	80 yd. Dash	M. Mathews	Oakgrove	10. sec	1953
	100 yd. Dash	E. Scherling	Woodstock	12.4 secs.	1946
	Broad Jump	E. Scherling	Woodstock	14ft 10 ins.	1946
	Hop-step Jump	E. Scherling	Woodstock	32ft 2½ ins.	194[illegible]
	High Jump	U. Kohli	Wynberg	4ft 6 ins.	1955
	Javelin Throw	E. Davenport	Wynberg	114ft 6 ins.	1954
	440 yd. Relay	—	Woodstock	58.1 secs.	1946
OPEN	100 yd. Dash	H. Duckstein	Woodstock	12.4 secs.	1953

The number of 'Railway children', whose parents had received generous hill-school educational assistance, fell as these entitlements were withdrawn from the mid-1950s. Also, with the age of retirement from the Railways reduced by three years, fewer parents could afford to send their children to hill-schools such as Wynberg-Allen on a full fee. Dwindling employment opportunities for Anglo-Indians in other sectors too, such as Posts & Telegraphs, meant greater call on either freeships or reduced fees. Seven years after Independence, the Annual Report mentions over 50% of the student body being Anglo-Indian. The dilemma facing the School was: to take in more needy Anglo-Indian children at reduced fee or, in the face of declining Government grants which would be further slashed from 1956, increase the numbers of full-paying boarders? Either ways, there were no easy answers.

We plough the fields, and scatter.
Matthias Claudius

All through the early-1950s, boys and girls from Wynberg-Allen continued to do well at the exams conducted by the Trinity College of Music, the London Royal Drawing Society, and other public bodies. While the Junior Cambridge examinations were abolished from 1953, the Senior Cambridge students continued to attain good results with the Cambridge Society taking especial note of the

WEDNESDAY 20th

	RED		GREEN
1.	T. Arnold (Oak Grove)	Pin Weight vs	N. DeQuadros (St. George's)
2.	J. Singh (St. George's)	Paper Weight vs	L. Swing (Allen)
3.	K. Souk (St. George's)	Gnat Weight vs	V. Aggarwal (Allen)
4.	L. Tocher (Oak Grove)	Midget Weight vs	I. Khan (Allen)
5.	R. White (St. George's)	Mosquito Weight vs	R. Bachman (Allen)
6.	N. Kakra (Oak Grove)	Fly Weight vs	H. Ahluwalia (St. George's)
		INTERVAL	
7.	R. Mallick (Oak Grove)	Bantam Weight vs	D. Bachman (Allen)
8.	P. Eyerson (Oak Grove)	Feather Weight vs	A. Cashmore (Allen)
9.	L. Camerson (Oak Grove)	Light Weight vs	L. Newnes (St. George's)
10.	D. Spencer (Oak Grove)	Welter Weight vs	K. Bachman (Allen)
11.	B. Tocher (Oak Grove)	Middle Weight vs	T. Dhatt
12.	P. Gill (St. George's)	Heav…	

Note: 4 - Ounce …

THURSDAY 21st

	RED		GREEN
1.	N. De Quadros (St. George's)	Pin Weight vs	H. Wong. (Allen)
2.	S. Burman (Oak Grove)	Paper Weight vs	J. Singh. (St. George's)
3.	Y. Goel (Oak Grove)	Gnat Weight vs	K. Souk. (St. George's)
4.	L. Tocher (Oak Grove)	Midget Weight vs	J. Ahlvwalia. (St. George's)
5.	G. Bhalla (Oak Grove)	Mosquito Weight vs	R. Bachman. (Allen)
6.	N. Kakra (Oak Grove)	Fly Weight vs	P. Yadav. (Allen)
		INTERVAL	
7.	C. Singh (St. George's)	Bantam Weight vs	D. Bachman. (Allen)
8.	R. Jaiswal (St. George's)	Feather Weight vs	A. Cashmore. (Allen)
9.	L. Cameron (Oak Grove)	Light Weight vs	R. Bince. (Allen)
10.	A. …	Welter Weight vs	K. Bachman. (Allen)
		Middle Weight vs	M. Sein. (Allen)
		Heavy Weight vs	P. S. Gill. (St. George's)

…ith a minute's rest up to mosquito

…nds with a minute's rest from Fly to Heavy

List of Events Completed Before Sports' Day

WYNBERG

Seniors
Broad Jump
High Jump
Javelin Throw

Intermediate
High Jump
Shot Putt
Basket Ball

Juniors
Broad Jump
Cricket Ball
Standing Broad Jump

Boys & Girls under 11
Broad Jump
Cricket Ball

Boys & Girls under 9
Flat Race

Under 8
Flat Race

Under 7
Potato Race

Babies under 6
Potato Race

ALLEN

Seniors
One Mile
Marathon
High Jump
Discus Throw
Javelin Throw
Pole Vault
Broad Jump
Shot Put
Hop, Step & Jump

Intermediate
Broad Jump
Hop Step & Jump
Shot Putt
Discus
Javelin
Pole Vault

Juniors
Marathon
High Jump
Pole Vault
Broad Jump

Sub-Juniors
High Jump
Cricket Ball Throw
Broad Jump

Preparatory
Cricket Ball Throw
Broad Jump

LORD BABS

Synopsis

Lord Drayford-Babs wishes to marry pretty but penniless Clara; he does so, but to overcome the objections of his Aunt, the Countess of Sawbridge, he keeps the secret from her and gets her to employ Clara as a parlour-maid.

Shortly after the wedding ceremony he is involved in a motor accident and to evade imprisonment enters into a conspiracy with his wife and a friend, Doctor Neville. The latter persuades Babs to play the part of a child and promises to explain that his actions are due to mental regression, following on shock. In his supposed treatment of the case, Dr. Neville is given ample opportunity to court and eventually to win the charming Lady Joan, niece of the countess.

Babs agrees to play the role of an infant, but the suspicions of the countess and of an interfering J.P., Sir Henry Buckby, complicate matters. The irate gentleman demands a pro-

THE CAST

(In order of their appearance)

Clara	...	Ivy Bootman.
Dr. Richard Neville	...	Jairam Asrani.
Lady Joan	...	Ruth Downes.
The Countess of Sawbridge	...	Terence Sterling.
Basil (Lord Drayford)	...	Olaf Craven.
Mr. Villiers	...	George Farmer.
Sir Henry Buckby, J.P.	...	Harold Hart.
Nurse Rounce.	...	Rodney Broughton.
Sir James Gumley M.D.	...	Surinder Rautela.
Producer	...	Terence Sterling.
Sound Effects, Lighting, Stage Manager	...	Lionel Maxwell-Pigott.
Prompter	...	Noel Thomas.
Make-up	...	Ouida Raymond & Beryl Sterling.
Scenery	...	Daphne Nestor.
Stage decoration	...	Doris Jobe.

Scene

... at Sawbridge Hall.

WYNBERG-ALLEN SWIMMING CARNIVAL - ON SATURDAY,13TH JUNE, 1959.

P R O G R A M M E O F E V E N T S:

1. 25 yds. Free Style ... Under 14 Boys.
2. 50 yds. Free Style ... Under 16 Boys.
3. 50 yds. Free Style ... OPENS Boys.
4. 25 yds. Breast Stroke ... Under 14 Boys.
5. 25 yds. Breast Stroke ... Under 16 Boys.
6. 50 yds. Breast Stroke ... OPENS Boys.
7. 25 yds. Back Stroke ... Under 16 Boys.
8. 50 yds. Back Stroke ... OPENS Boys.
9. Diving ... Under 16 Boys.

I N T E R V A L

10. Plunging ... OPENS Boys.
11. Diving ... Under 14 Boys.
12. Diving ... OPENS Boys.
13. Under Water ... OPENS Boys.
14. Free Style Relay (4 x 1) Boys.
15. Medley Relay (3 x 1) Boys.
16. Staff Vs Boys Free Style Relay.

****

****

****

O F F I C I A L

1. TIME KEEPERS: Mr. Kidd. Mr. Reading.
2. FINISH JUDGES: Mr. Abbott. Mr. T. Jobe. Mr. Sharma.
3. DIVING JUDGES: Mr. Marklew. Mr. Craven. Mr. Phillips.
4. REFEREE: Major Cunnington.
5. ANNOUNCER: Mr. Geyer.
6. STARTER: Mr. Phillips.
7. MARSHAL: Mr. Bernard.
8. RECORDER: Mr. Kamboh.
9. ORGANIZER: Mr. Phillips and Mr. Marklew.

DISTRIBUTION OF TROPHIES:

Mrs. Cunnington.

FIRST - BLUE - 16.
SECOND- RED - 10.
THIRD - GREEN- 6.
FOURTH- YELLOW- 4.

RELAYS DOUBLE POINTS

performance of the Wynberg-Allen students showing a 100% pass result year after year. However, from 1954, the U.P. government brought in the 11-year school course (including the two years of Upper KG and Lower KG); consequently, the Senior Cambridge Examination was taken in Class IX instead of Class X. This had two immediate effects: one, the loss of Class X (averaging 24 students) meant loss of tuition fees and a consequent reduction of Maintenance Grant; and two, the internal examination conducted at Class VIII became a screening test of sorts. Also, as per government orders, a compulsory Hindi exam had to be cleared towards the end of Class VIII. With the shortening of the school years from 12 to 11, the Government allowed students from all the Anglo-Indian schools in the U.P. to take at the end of Class VIII, if they so desired, the U.P. High School Examination. However, disparities between the two 'systems' of education, their differing standards and curricula did not always make this a viable option. Muddying the waters further was the agitation for teaching in the vernacular that was gaining ground in different parts of the country. Consequently, there was fear in some quarters as to the viability of education in Anglo-Indian schools and whether, and to what extent, they would equip Indian students for higher education in Indian colleges and universities. On the other hand, more and more Indian parents wanted an English-medium education for their children. Confusion was compounded as culture, identity, politics and education came together to form a bitter cocktail.

At this difficult juncture, the scattered family of old boys and girls wrote from different parts of India and from Pakistan, England, Australia, Ceylon, Africa, and America pledging support and upholding the 'spirit of Wynberg'. Some worked in the Indian Administrative Services, or held positions from the secretarial to the highest in the air force, navy, army and police; others worked in banks and churches and hospitals as well as plantations and private enterprises. Many wanted to send their own children to their alma mater; others visited the old school and offered help in myriad ways. The Wards of the Society — the orphans and destitutes who had been directed to Wynberg-Allen through the good offices of the church or community elders and had not merely found a safe haven but also kindly mentors — had gone on to do equally well; some were settled in England, others found training as nurses or joined the Army. An advertisement, taken out in 1954, announced Wynberg-Allen as 'the official institution for children of the Survey of India in this area'; this assured an additional flow of new pupils.

Elizabeth Davenport, 1953.

A steady stream of successes continued to be reported from different fields. Three lads from Allen made it to the National Defence Academy in 1952. One Wynberg lass, Elizabeth 'Jumbo' Davenport, beat by a wide margin the long-standing All-India Women's record for the Javelin Throw in 1954.[8] Neil Todd of Allen gained the distinction of becoming the personal pilot of Pandit Nehru. And, Saeed 'Joff' Jaffrey, joined the All India Radio as an Announcer and Commentator before embarking on a stage career in the UK.[9] Some other Old Boys who were doing well in their chosen fields included: Minoo Dinshaw (Senior Cambridge batch of 1939) who joined the Indian Navy and went on to command the I.N.S. 'Shakti'; Edgar Nelson (1944-50) who went on to study medicine at Harvard; Ian Loughran who became an honorary flying instructor at the Delhi Gliding Club and set a new gliding record for Asia. The summer of 1956 saw the opening of a magnificent swimming pool, the fruition of a dream of many an Old Boy fighting in the deserts of West Asia during the last War, and whose contributions had formed the nucleus of a 'Memorial Fund' that made their dream come true.

[8] She went on to bring honours to the School when, in the Asian Games in Tokyo in 1958, she was placed Second in the Javelin Throw and was selected to represent India in the Empire Games at Cardiff later the same year.
[9] Saeed Jaffrey's autobiography, *Saeed: An Actor's Journey* (Harper Collins, 1999), carries an affectionate account of his years at Bala.

Mr P. A. Kidd.

On 15 November 1957, the School bid farewell to Rev and Mrs Biggs. It was a time of sunshine and showers, joy mixed with sadness. For 17 years, their home on the School premises, 'Windyridge', had held out a ready welcome for any member of the School community. But there was comfort in knowing that the new incumbent, Mr P. A. Kidd, a man with an 'almost embarrassing wealth of commendation' in the field of academia, administration and education, was a worthy successor. His arrival was fortuitous; at a time when the School was preparing to change itself to the new higher secondary system of education, with his impeccable qualifications, Kidd brought a wealth of practical experience, and coming from New South Wales, Australia, also a whiff of internationalism.

Possibly taking a cue from a statement made by A. C. Grice, Anglo-Indian Member of the U.P. Assembly to increase enrolments in Anglo-Indian schools in order to successfully face the problems resulting from the loss of Government grants which fully came into effect from 1960, Kidd unleashed a wave of fresh enrolments. In his first year itself, numbers rose from 300 to 350 and 370 the next year; by 1960 they swelled to 400. The hiring of overseas staff (mostly missionaries who received exactly the same salaries as the Indian staff) boosted school life in many ways: of course, the standard of teaching improved; co-curricular activities too received a shot in the arm. With Kidd actively advertising Wynberg-Allen as a modern school modelled on the lines of a 'public school', meant primarily for Anglo-Indian children but warmly welcoming of children of all denominations and nationalities, students from Indonesia, Thailand, China, Burma, Japan, Afghanistan, East Africa, Canada and England began to settle in along with their Indian peers.

The early 1960s were a period of strife and turmoil for the country. War clouds loomed on the eastern and western front; strikes and farmers' agitation tore the peace of cities and villages alike; campuses became veritable hotbeds of political unrest. New movements for regional autonomy threatened the unity of India and the spectre of Balkanisation loomed large. The hills of Upper India were alive to the call of separate statehood, a demand that would peak in the late 1990s as the clamour for the creation of a new State, Uttarakhand, reached a crescendo. In the midst of all this turmoil, one fact emerged with absolute clarity: more and more parents wanted to send their children to the so-called 'Anglo-Indian' schools, for they were convinced that they offered a happy mix of sports-education-co-curricular activities in a salubrious environment. This was evident from the fact that in 1960, for the first time in its history, Wynberg-Allen had a waiting list from KG onwards!

The School saw a sudden influx of Tibetan and Mongolian refugee children in 1962-63; to support them, the Methodist young people of Australia, through the World Council of Churches in Geneva, sent a gift of £650 and, to house them, the National Christian Council of India bought a suitable building for Rs. 27,000. The Committee for American Relief Everywhere (CARE) offered Rs. 13,000 to fully equip the building for the new inmates. The idea of taking in Tibetan refugee children was first mooted by the Evangelical Alliance Mission who, moved by the plight of Tibetans who had flocked to Mussoorie in 1960, offered to pay Rs. 24,000 per year and also lent the services of two experienced missionaries, Miss Stam and Miss Norman, to supervise the Tibetan Hostel attached to the School. It must be recalled that it was in March 1959 that the 23-year old Dalai Lama had first set up his government-in-exile in Happy Valley (from Gadenling, meaning 'happy valley' in Tibetan), Mussoorie before moving on to Dharamshala in Himachal Pradesh. In 1962, the Tibetan Homes Foundation had been set up to take care of the many Tibetan children left homeless or orphaned on the long march from Lhasa to Mussoorie, and to serve as a repository of Tibetan culture, language, religion and way of life. While the first school for Tibetans on Indian soil, the Central School for Tibetans, inaugurated by the Dalai Lama on 3 March 1960, served the educational needs of many, it was

His Holiness the Dalai Lama on a visit to the School, 1960.

Facing page: Mrs Warren at a presentation ceremony, 1966. Below: Mr C. M. Macmillan.

towards established schools such as Wynberg-Allen that this fledgling community of exiles looked for guidance and support. By the end of 1963, 61 Tibetan children had joined the Wynberg community; one of them, Champa Dhakpa (nicknamed 'Champa the Champ' for the number of prizes he collected!), is the much-loved coach and popular figure on the School campus.

Meanwhile, a new form of examination, known as the Indian School Certificate Examination, was introduced in 1963; this made General Science and Social Studies compulsory for all students. To make the sharing of resources more equitable, the School changed over completely to co-education the same year. This necessitated the reduction of 'Houses' from eight in both schools to four, namely: Powell, Condon, Foy and Allen. The 75th Anniversary celebrations on 27 May 1964 were presided over by Rev Biggs who had been induced to come out of retirement as interim Principal; on behalf of the Wynberg community he bid farewell to Mr Kidd who had returned to Australia after a tragic accident and welcomed Malcolm Macmillan, also from New South Wales.[10]

The year 1965 dealt a severe blow to the School. A kindly guiding light, a loving benefactress and faithful friend passed away. This was 'Our Mrs Allen', wife of Henry Allen, a lady who had nurtured the School named after her husband from afar, made frequent trips across the seas to check on its well-being, and lavished it with many big and small gestures of benevolence. Long years ago, on 22 November 1927, she had laid the foundation stone for the Henry Allen Memorial School with a plaque bearing the inscription:

[10] Mr Kidd's tenure was marked by several significant turns, namely: record high enrolments which began to show adversely in over-crowded dorms and poor exam results; the introduction of two diets and two areas in the dining room (a practice that was fortunately discontinued by his successors); and a steady stream of overseas staff that complemented the Indian teachers. Mr Kidd met with a serious accident while driving the School van, filled with several staff members, on 17 July 1963. The van fell down the hill near the Wynberg gate causing serious injuries to its passengers and especially grave ones to Mr Kidd who had to return to Australia. In the interim, till a new Principal could be found, Rev Biggs filled the breach.

Junior School Staff, 1965.

For the glory of Christ and the blessing of His little ones and in memory of one of His servants who loved the children for His sake

True to the words of the inscription, she — on behalf of her husband — continued to love the children housed at Wynberg-Allen for the Lord's sake. She and her husband had first visited the School — then a small co-educational institution mostly for orphans and indigent children — while they were on their honeymoon and staying in a house near Oaks Road. Soon, the newly-weds took to dropping in at Wynberg and making friends with the boys and girls studying there. Henry Allen began by taking the occasional Children's Service and found that he — not to say his young audience — enjoyed it so much that it became a weekly ritual. Soon the Allens were completely drawn into the activities of the small community at Wynberg with Henry serving on the Board. Her married life cut unexpectedly short, Mrs Allen decided to

1966 Founders' Day Guests Mr A. E. T. Barrow, M.P., Mr A. C. Grice, M.L.A., Dr G. D. Lehmann, with Mr C. M. Macmillan.

take up her husband's mission to work for the betterment of the school. When her husband died, his brother wanted to put up a stained glass window in his memory at the family church in Mashobra. But Mrs Allen declined; she wanted something more than a stained glass window. Years later, on the Founders' Day Service of 8 October 1947, she narrated this incident and looking down at the hall full of boys and girls, said she did not want a stained glass window in a church in memory of her late husband; instead, she wanted 'a living memorial'. The Allen School was indeed a living memorial, and a fitting one, one that she tended with all the resources at her command. That she did so for over four decades with neither dip nor deviation is a testament to her devotion. Rev Biggs, quite rightly, described Mrs Allen's wonderful love for the School as a 'link between God's grace and our need'. And it is only appropriate that, today when we look back, we count her and her husband among the founders of the School and instead of the original quartet we can say that there were six and not four founders.

1968-1988

TESTING
THE METTLE
The Years of
Struggle and Strife

Ye have not been this way heretofore.
Joshua 3:4

The Report of the Education Commission of 1964-66 (the Kothari Commission) had stated:

> In the rapidly changing world of today, one thing is certain: yesterday's educational system will not meet today's and even less so, the demands of tomorrow...

Indeed, the times...they were a'changing and with the changing times, not just Wynberg-Allen but all schools were perforce undergoing change. In fact, the whole education system in the country was going through a period of transition from the old one laid down in Macaulay's Minutes to a new one that would be in tune with the new demands of a secular, democratic nation-state. Changes were being wrought in the curriculum, especially in the field of science and mathematics. Even English had to be taught in an entirely new way to pupils who came from non-English speaking homes. What is more, at Wynberg-Allen, the steady influx of missionaries who had constituted the bulk of the overseas staff began to dwindle by the dawn of the seventies.[1] Increasingly, the School found itself relying almost entirely on native resources to teach native children.[2]

As the country celebrated its twentieth year of freedom from British rule, the School took stock of its fortunes. The prophets of doom and disaster who had foretold the end of Christian schools and even English-medium education were found to be wrong. More Indian parents wanted to send their children to such schools than to the many other new English-medium schools that were mushrooming all over the country. In fact, more parents preferred English-medium education despite the many fallacies perpetuated by the 'Hindi Imperialists' who advocated the blanket imposition of the national language as the de facto and exclusive medium of instruction. Far from being confined to a linguistic minority, English had emerged as a link language, a modern-day *lingua franca* as it were.The grim forebodings about the future

[1] There were several much-loved foreign staff during this period; some of them were: Mr Jeremy Firth and Mr Colin Carr who taught English; Miss Joan Millson who taught Geography and Scripture; Miss Elaine Lovell who worked in the Tibetan Hostel; Miss Pat Grauss, Miss Beryl Norman, Miss Dorothy Leslie, Barry and Wilma McNicoll who taught in the Primary School; Ruth Cummings who worked as Supervisor in the Wynberg Hostel.

[2] The Report for July 1969, filed by R. C. Tiwari, Inspector of Anglo-Indian Schools, Nainital, U.P., states that of the 512 students on roll, 16 boys and 18 girls belong to the Anglo-Indian community. 'As such, attention has now been diverted to the large section of children belonging to other communities as well.' Of the 512 students, 57 were free, 150 on half fee.

of institutions that were regarded as 'Raj relics' and targets of public ire and even abuse too proved to be false. As did the apprehension that even if Schools such as Wynberg-Allen, with its specifically British legacy, were to survive would they be able to maintain their Christian character? What is more, with the rapidly dwindling Anglo-Indian community in India, whose interests would they serve? Twenty years later, most of these questions were satisfactorily answered and many of these apprehensions were laid to rest. For, clearly, Wynberg-Allen had not merely survived in the past two decades but flourished — in spite of the political, economic and, to some extent, religious right-wing pressures. As the number of Anglo-Indian pupils declined, the School had opened its door to the 'Nationals' clamouring for admission — Hindu, Muslim, Sikh and Christian. It had been a good neighbour and a Good Samaritan by admitting a large number of children from the Tibetan refugees who had come to these mountains in search of a safe haven from Chinese oppression. And, like the Church of India, the School too had accepted the changes that were inevitable and girded itself to face new responsibilities in the belief that 'We know not what the future holds; we know *who* holds the future.'

On the School's 80th Founders' Day on 24 May 1968, the guest of honour, Mr S. C. Jamir, Deputy Minister of Labour, Employment and Rehabilitation, drew the school's attention to another small community in a distant part of the country, the Nagas. Exhorting the students in rousing words, he gave the example of the Nagas who had undergone a transformation:

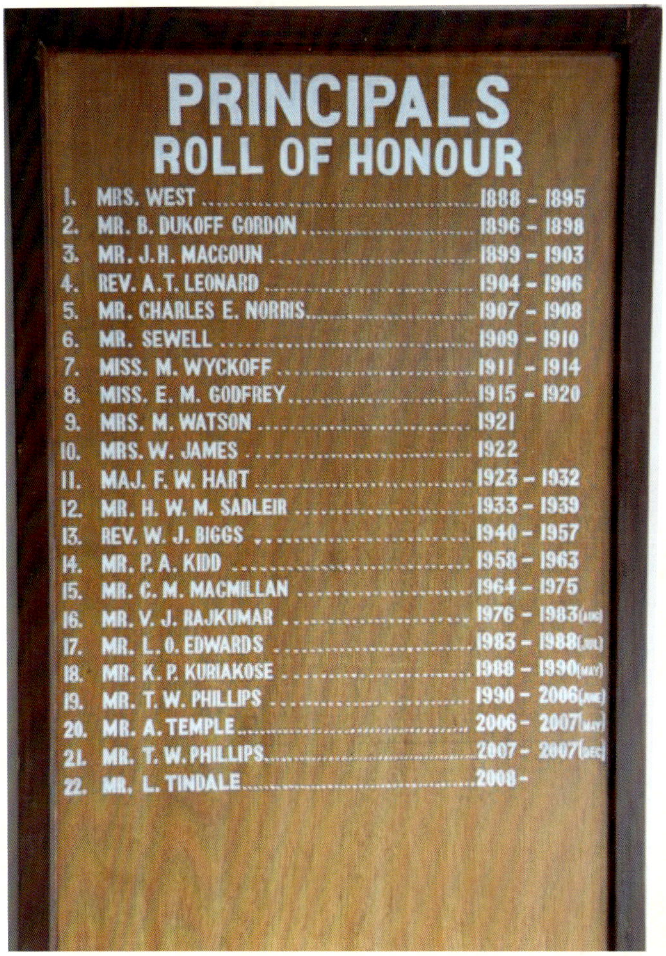

> Small communities when inspired by powerful ideas and fired by ennobling aspirations, are capable of opening new chapters in the history of mankind, and in the process Christianity has helped in uniting the Nagas into one strong and powerful community meriting a lasting existence and recognition.

On the same occasion, Rev Biggs, in his capacity as Principal Emeritus, described the School as *Nulli Secundus* ('Second to None') and spoke of the School's new role in a new India in the following words:

> Here proudly stands Wynberg-Allen that once served mainly a foreign people and their descendants, but now is intimately integrated with the needs and ambitions of this wide-flung, throbbing-nation Bharat and her people over the seas.

Persisting to use the answers of yesterday to solve the problems of today would result in the world passing us by, wrote Mr Macmillan in his school report. When the first man set foot on the moon in July 1969, what struck him most forcefully — he reminded his audience — was not the vastness of the lunar landscape but the smallness of the world as we know it; seen from the moon the earth seemed so small, so puny. The Psalm, too, tells the Believers that looking and perceiving is a matter of perspective:

Daffodils in bloom.

When I look at Thy heavens, the work of Thy fingers,
The moon and the stars which Thou hast established;
What is man that Thou art mindful of him
And the son of man that Thou dost care for him?

Psalm 8:3 & 4

These words could just as well be interpreted to mean that traditional approaches and answers would no longer do at a time when the questions themselves had changed. The challenge was to come to terms with the science and technology of the modern age and yet be mindful of the God of the heavens. Equally, the challenge was to accept this paradox and demonstrate it in the running of the school, in caring equally for all of God's creatures: the rich and poor, the dull as well as clever, the privileged as well as the disempowered. Put succinctly, the challenge was:

> We who would follow Christ in the Space Age must be prepared to comprehend a new order of learning and of science together with the greatest of human values which we know as LOVE.

This emphasis on a Christian education was to remain right up till the mid-1970s. Possibly this was as much to keep the forces of materialism at bay as to inculcate an interest in religion per se. The School saw its task as providing an all-rounded education. 'To know a little less and to understand a little more' seemed to be the mantra. At the same time, the School's guiding principle till this point did not mean providing a good academic education with a bit of Christianity 'tacked on'; if anything, it meant a form of education that was Christian through and through, in its aims, contents and methods. It meant providing students with the key to that philosophy which is the gospel of Jesus Christ. In the words of an old hymn, 'Christ is our cornerstone/On him alone we build...'

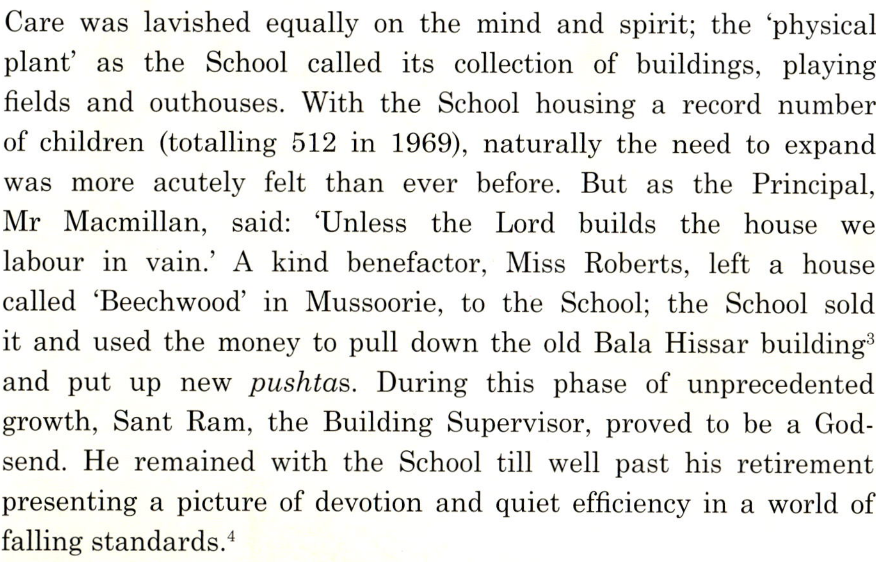

Care was lavished equally on the mind and spirit; the 'physical plant' as the School called its collection of buildings, playing fields and outhouses. With the School housing a record number of children (totalling 512 in 1969), naturally the need to expand was more acutely felt than ever before. But as the Principal, Mr Macmillan, said: 'Unless the Lord builds the house we labour in vain.' A kind benefactor, Miss Roberts, left a house called 'Beechwood' in Mussoorie, to the School; the School sold it and used the money to pull down the old Bala Hissar building[3] and put up new *pushta*s. During this phase of unprecedented growth, Sant Ram, the Building Supervisor, proved to be a God-send. He remained with the School till well past his retirement presenting a picture of devotion and quiet efficiency in a world of falling standards.[4]

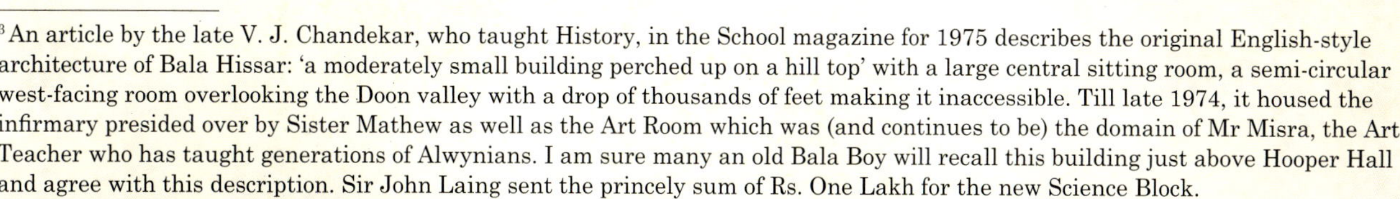

[3] An article by the late V. J. Chandekar, who taught History, in the School magazine for 1975 describes the original English-style architecture of Bala Hissar: 'a moderately small building perched up on a hill top' with a large central sitting room, a semi-circular west-facing room overlooking the Doon valley with a drop of thousands of feet making it inaccessible. Till late 1974, it housed the infirmary presided over by Sister Mathew as well as the Art Room which was (and continues to be) the domain of Mr Misra, the Art Teacher who has taught generations of Alwynians. I am sure many an old Bala Boy will recall this building just above Hooper Hall and agree with this description. Sir John Laing sent the princely sum of Rs. One Lakh for the new Science Block.

[4] Sant Ram served for over six decades. In the course of an interview, Mr Terence Phillips recalled for me Sant Ram's diligence and devotion to the School as also his near-photographic recall of which building was built when at what cost. I found a one-page article written by Sant Ram himself in the School magazine for the year 1983. Among the many feathers in his cap was the Recreation Block, completed in June 1972; it comprised a common room, lounge, quiet room, tuck-shop as well as changing rooms and toilets and a gymnasium complete with a wooden floor. It was built with contributions from the late Mrs Allen's three daughters as well as her grandchildren and a legacy from Miss Tessa Dickson.

Mr. Sant Ram—A Legend

I was born on 13th November 1904 in the village of Brahmi, P.O. Sarsawa, District Saharanpur, U. P. My family's hereditary occupation has been carpentry and agriculture. I grazed cattle up to the age of 10 years. Then after learning a little Urdu my brother took me to Saharanpur and had me admitted in class III in a Govt. school. English was compulsory from 3rd standard and all the subjects were taught in English in those days. I studied in this school up to class 8 having a scholarship of Rs 4/- per month for 4 years, standing 1st or 2nd in classes IV, V, VI and VII and paid school fees of Rs. 1/- per month.

I was weak in free hand drawing, so I left this school and joined Govt. C. O. High School Roorkee, where I took mathematics as my optional subject instead of drawing. From this school I passed the S. L. C. Examination in April 1922.

My father was fifty years older than me so I had to seek work to maintain my family. I worked for 13 months in carriage and wagon Department in N. W. R. Saharanpur as an Assistant Train Examiner. Then I worked with my brother as a workman who was I. O. W in N. W. R. posted on frontier side, now in Pakistan.

In July 1928 I came to Mussoorie with my father-in-law who was working as a contractor with Hart & Co. a building agency run by: Mr. A. E. Hart.
Mr. F. W. Hart
Mr. F. W. Roberts

Retired Engineers: A. E. Hart was an active member of Hart & Co. and F. W. Hart was the Superintendent of Wynberg Homes Society—who built the Henry Allen Memorial School in 1927-1930.

It was Mr. A. E. Hart who taught me all this work which I have been doing up till now. In May 1932 he sent me to Major F. W. Hart who appointed me as a carpenter on Rs 60/-.

Then Mr. Sadlier came as the school principal—who later became the Inspector of Anglo-Indian Schools. In his time the Hart Memorial building was built. Mr. Durga Dutt and Mr. Sadlier the Principal brought me from the servants register to the staff register and named me as a building supervisor My pay for the 25 months during the course of construction of the 'Hart memorial' was Rs 100/- per month in 1938-1940.

In Mr. Biggs time there was very little work. Only the staff club room and the library was built. School was registered as an orphanage and funds were limited. My pay was Rs. 60/- per month and I could hardly get Rs 26/- worth of material per month for maintenance work. So on 21st August 1949 I left the school work and went back to my village and carried on my farm work.

Then in Sept. 1982 Mr. Biggs and Mr. Kidd called me back. Since then, the following buildings have been constructed: Alwyn in Wynberg, Gymnnsium, Recreation Block, Science Block, New Kitchen and the new class rooms which are still under construction.

I have only one son, who was educated from the earnings of Wynberg-Allen school and who has come up to the rank of Suprintendent Engineer. By the grace of God I have still kept the ancestral property in my village though there have been many upheavals such as the Zamindars Abolition and Ceiling Act. I therefore owe a great deal of debt to Wynberg Allen School, its members and all those Principals, more than half a dozen, who helped me to carry out my duties.

—Sant Ram

[50]

WAYSIDE COTTAGE

The School's new Land Rover, a gift from Sir John Laing, 1970.

A fine new four-storied building, called the Alwyn Building, had already come up in Wynberg in May 1968. Its construction was made possible through the generous gift of Pounds 12,000 by Sir John Laing of England. A new staff lounge, furnished by the kindness of Dr and Mrs Lehmann, came to be called the Lehmann lounge. A large property called 'Wayside' had been bought from the Powell family in 1966; while the Wayside Cottage was used as staff quarters, the adjacent grounds of the Wayside Hall Estate served as additional space for a sports field. 'Seven Oaks', too, was purchased from the remaining Powell descendent, Miss May Caroline Powell, in December 1974 and adapted for staff quarters. The rambling, large old house, a cottage plus outhouses situated on 30 acres of land would prove to be an asset in the years to come; what is more standing as it does between the two schools, 'Seven Oaks' provided a much-needed link corridor. The stately Deodars and Himalayan Oaks growing tall and majestic on its compound added to the School's natural beauty. With its

addition, the School now had a campus of 140 acres with well-defined boundaries, though regrettably the Mussoorie-Ambala Bypass built on the old bridle path to Rajpur sliced through the school property, dividing it in two unequal halves.

The earlier Seven Oaks.

The number of enrolments continued to hover around 510 or so all through the early 1970s with approximately 400 boarders. The only significant trend appeared to be an increasing number of enquiries from Indian parents living in England who had heard good things about Wynberg-Allen and wished to send their children to be educated in India. Possibly due to the rampant use of drugs and alcohol in Western schools and the rising level of indiscipline and immorality in co-educational boarding schools elsewhere, a School such as Wynberg-Allen which prided itself on its strong Christian values and emphasis on healthy living, held out obvious attractions for parents.

Major Harsh Bahuguna (above) with Tenzing Norgay (facing page).
Below: Bala Hissar before and after demolition (facing page).

In April 1971, an illustrious Old Boy who had brought many a laurel to the School, Major Harsh Bahuguna (School Captain of 1954), was tragically killed while on an international expedition to Mount Everest. Born in the Garhwal hills, he had joined the Indian Military Academy in 1956 and was commissioned in the Armoured Corps in 1958. In 1962, after a course in mountaineering from the Himalayan Mountaineering Institute in Darjeeling under the legendary Tenzing Norgay, he joined the successful expedition to Leo Porgial in 1963, Nanda Devi in 1964 and Mt Everest in 1965. Appointed Instructor at the Indian Military Academy in Dehra Dun, Major Bahuguna became a frequent visitor to his old school. In paying a tribute to his memory, the School recalled these lines from Lawrence Binyon:

> He shall not grow old, as we that are left grow old;
> Age shall not weary him, nor the years condemn.
> At the going down of the sun and in the morning
> We will remember him.

And indeed, the School did remember him — by naming its new Science Block in his memory. The oldest building at Allen, Bala Hissar, which had housed Dost Mohammad during his years of exile and which the School had bought in 1919, was pulled down in 1975 to make way for the new Harsh Bahuguna Science Block. Laying its Foundation Stone on 16 November 1975, the Chairman, Dr G. D. Lehmann urged his listeners thus: 'If you have got money that you don't need, or money that you *do* need but you feel we need more, well send it in to the Bahuguna Memorial Fund and you'll see our Science Block spring up!' And, indeed, like much of the building activity at Wynberg-Allen since its inception, it did come up due to the generosity of friends and well-wishers.

The old order changeth yielding place to new
And God fulfils himself in many ways
Lest one good custom should corrupt the world.

'The Passing of Arthur' by Alfred Tennyson

Mr Durga Datt Pantha

When I came to the Wynberg-Allen school as Principal in 1940 Mr Durga Datt Pantha had already been in the School Office as Accountant for eight years (3 years with Major Hart and 5 years with Mr Sadleir). This was succeeded by a further 18 years with me and then for further 5 years with Mr Kidd. He was the mainstay of the Office — indeed in one way, of the whole School, and his is a wonderful record of truly dedicated service.

To him parents went; through him all supplies were arranged for the Principal; he was the school diplomatic envoy — staff, parents, children and hostel workers. He showed to all in this service a complete sense of responsibility and his integrity was never questioned by anyone. He was the first to arrive at work and the last to leave, and often his light was seen burning in the office at half-past nine at night. On his journal I found pasted this couplet which was his guiding principle in all his life service:

> Work as if thou must die today
> Pray as if thou must live for aye.

In all of my own 18 years of service I never knew him to take a holiday even on persuasion, save once when the Board insisted he should have time off from work, when he had two weeks away from the office.

My friend, Durga Datt, was of undaunted courage, as was seen in the 1947 upheaval, when though a Brahmin of the highest order, he sheltered 17 Moslem school servants in the main office, himself sleeping across the entrance door, till they could be removed to the refugee camp.

I knew of no man who was held in such high esteem by all classes and creeds. I never knew him to lose his temper or his patience and I personally was more than once saved by his wisdom from justified but foolish action.

It was with real grief and a sense of deep loss that we learned on the 4th of November 1975 of the call of this truly great gentleman amongst us.

W. J. Biggs
Principal Emeritus

Major F. W. Hart Memorial Building.

Shortly thereafter, Mr Macmillan left the School after 12 eventful years at the helm to be replaced by the first ever Indian principal, Mr V. J. Rajkumar on 16 December 1975. For the first time in the 87 years of its existence, the School's principalship was offered to a 'native'. A fine sportsman, a double M.A. in English and American literature as well as a B. Ed, Mr Rajkumar had served in the N.C.C. and the I.A.F. before serving as a Master at the Sainik School in Korukonda (Andhra Pradesh) and as Principal of Stewart School in Bhubhaneshwar (Orissa). In keeping with the 10+2+3 formula introduced by the Ministry of Education, the School proposed the beginning of a new Standard XII, though it wouldn't be till 1977 that the first batch actually came into existence with 11 intrepid students braving snow and ice to take the first-ever Class XII examination on 1 March 1978.

The year 1977 took away two people who had served the School most assiduously: Mrs Biggs, mother to the scores upon scores of Alwynians who had known and loved her as 'Mama Biggs', passed away on 15 May 1977 at the age of 88 years. Likening her to Deborah, a mother in Israel who, according to Judges, had been raised of God to be a ruler, Dr Lehmann said: 'Many a woman have done excellently but you surpass them all.' (Prov. 31:29). Her husband, Rev Biggs, lonely after her death, expressed a wish to go back to his home in Rainham, Essex. Rev Cornelius of the Union Church, escorted him

Union Church, Mussoorie.

COURTESY: LAZARUS CORNELIUS

to London, but Rev Biggs fell ill and died in a hospital in Southend on 10 November, a few weeks after his return from India. The passing away of 'Papa Biggs', Principal Emeritus, marked the end of an era. A man of rare financial acumen as well as spiritual resources, he carried the School single-handedly through the most turbulent years of its history. Were it not for his strong hands at the helm of affairs, Wynberg-Allen may well have capsized and sunk in the troubled waters of post-Independence India.

Members of the Christian community in Mussoorie continued to take an active interest in the School. Rev Cornelius and his wife threw themselves whole-heartedly into the school's activities, both religious and lay. While the Reverend came by to speak to the Senior students every Wednesday, his wife took Scripture classes for the Junior children every Thursday. Their active ministry in the School continues till this day as does Rev Cornelius's rousing, passionate sermons during Sunday service. Ralston Manor Hostel, which had housed the Tibetan students, was closed down in 1978; instead a new hostel was constructed at Wynberg to accommodate the Junior school boys. The School bought Maplewood Lodge from Miss Gordon for Rs 20,000 in 1979; it was used to accommodate the growing numbers of staff members. The staff position by 1980 stood at a robust 53 with 48 Christians, 7 British, 11 Anglo-Indians, 4 Hindus and 1 Tibetan. The overseas community of old students and well-wishers continued to support the School with the Panahpur Charitable Trust sending £3,000 and the Sir John Laing Trust contributing £8,000 for constructing new classrooms in Allen. Apart from constructing a new academic block for the Senior School, work had begun on another major project: to draw water from the abundant natural springs on the School's own property that would cure once and for all the chronic water shortage, especially in the summers.

A specifically Christian club called the Salt Club had been in existence since the 1970s. The Club would meet every Sunday afternoon for singing, fellowship and to learn from God's word. Taking its inspiration from Matthew's Gospel which says, 'Ye are the salt of the earth, but if the salt have lost his savour, wherewith shall it be salted?' it took

The old swimming pool that was there till the mid-nineties.

upon itself the onerous task of spreading the Word of God. Like much else in the School, it had no proselytising intent; it welcomed both Christian and non-Christian students but made no attempt at evangelising or conversion. Its activities included putting up skits and conducting assemblies at School and at the Union Church. On one occasion, its members visited a camp for the blind at Deodars in Happy Valley; on another they attended a two-day camp conducted by Miss C. Blunt, the leader of the Club, which included games, quizzes, skits and Bible Study groups. Its members took renewed interest in the Club's activities under the supervision of Mr Richard Viney, the Physics teacher who joined the School in 1979 from the U.K.

Socially Useful Productive Work (SUPW), made mandatory by the Ministry of Education from 1978, saw the senior students helping out at the hospital under the supervision of Mrs Viney. SUPW, meant to inculcate Gandhian values in students, fostered a sense of community service among senior students from

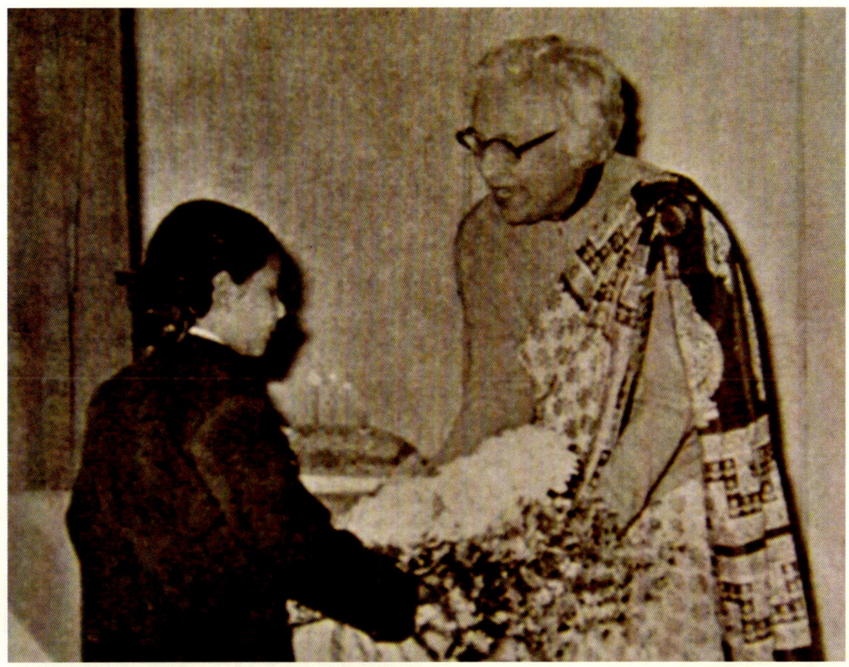

Guest of Honour Mrs Vijaylakshmi Pandit at the Fancy Fair, 1971.

Class IX onwards. A Humanities and Commerce stream was introduced for Classes XI-XII from 1983. By 1984, the School was showing a record enrolment of 856 students (with almost 250 in the past year itself!); of these 624 were boarders. The student-staff ratio in the Junior School stood at 24:1 and for the Seniors at a healthy16:1.The student community was drawn from across the world with 171 students from 15 different countries.

Remove not the ancient landmarks.

Prov 22:28

While at one level, it was business as usual at Wynberg-Allen, at another level the problems that had been setting in for some time, had begun to eat away at the one singular quality that the school had always prided itself in, namely Discipline. A growing insubordination and disrespect for authority began to mar the even tenor of the School that had been so carefully nurtured by men like Rev Biggs and Mr Macmillan. Pride and love for the institution, always the hallmark of both staff and students alike at Wynberg-Allen, fell prey to forces of anarchy and despondency. In 1983, Mr L. O. Edwards, who had joined Allen as Headmaster in 1965 and spent a 12-year stint in Florida to re-join in 1982, took over the running of the School from Mr Rajkumar. With his long innings both as a teacher and administrator and healthy regard for the 'spirit' of Wynberg, Edwards initiated a series of reforms and made a valiant effort to inject a healthy dose of morale boosters. Primarily, all those engaged in undermining the influence and authority of the Principal needed to be weeded out and fresh enthusiasm had to be re-injected for all that had once symbolised the Best of Wynberg-Allen: a demanding and rigorous games programmes, incentives to rejuvenate the flagging spirit of competitiveness and renewed academic vigour that could be seen in better examination results. Duty Rosters had to be implemented to the last detail and any compromise with discipline had to be non-negotiable.

Facing page: Mr L. O. Edwards with his wife Dorcas.

The Allen Gymnasium under construction, 1971.

Rev Albert W. Bowdish, taking over the Chairmanship in 1985 from the indefatigable Dr Lehmann (who had served the School dearly and well for 37 years and who would henceforth remain the 'Chairman Emeritus'), reminded the School that the price of liberty must be eternal vigilance. While peace and stability had been restored on the campus, he prayed to the Lord to keep the School 'ever alert, and to be sensitive to, and aware of the need for improvements, corrections, and progress'. While the School could draw some measure of solace at having recovered its poise by means of an exercise not unlike the cleaning of the Augean Stables, it could not afford to be sanguine; nor could the staff and administration rest on their oars. A considerably increased student body (a whopping 950 in 1985) and the recovery of old debts from defaulting parents meant that the School's coffers had filled up; however, more students meant a space crunch in terms of facilities and accommodation.

Having regained a degree of stability and contained the rampant unrest that had marred the last few years, the School now embarked upon the Herculean task of building and expanding its infrastructure. A slew of renovations, additions and construction activities were initiated: extensions in the kitchens, toilets, servants' quarters, dining halls, staff quarters, Junior library, a new gymnasium and playfield *pushta* for

Juniors and a brand-new auditorium. Much of this frenzied building and renovation work was being targeted for the Centenary Celebrations scheduled for June 1988. A Centenary Committee, under the chairmanship of Lt Col M. A. R. Skinner, was entrusted with the task of drawing up plans. Every effort was being made to elicit funds and donations to meet the anticipated high expenditure. Appeals were made through posters, circulars, notifications and newspaper announcements. In the winter of 1986, Principal Edwards, accompanied by the Office Superintendent, Mr P. A. Varghese, embarked on a fund-raising trip to Thailand to solicit generous contributions from Thai entrepreneurs of Indian origin who had been sending their children to Wynberg-Allen for several decades.

Several small but significant events happened during the run-up to the Centenary. A tidy sum of Rs. 18 lakh was collected for the Centenary fund through strenuous fund-raising activities from old students, well-wishers and the public at large. Congratulatory messages began to pour in: from Shri Venkataraman, the President of India; Rajiv Gandhi, the Prime Minister of India; General Sundarji, the Chief of Army Staff; Margaret Thatcher, the Prime Minster of Great Britain; His Holiness the Dalai Lama; as well as ministers, statesmen, and politicians of all hues. Mr Edwards' tenure as principal was extended to see the School through its hundredth-year celebrations. Meanwhile, enrolments had inched their way to cross the four-digit bar and stood at a record 1,100 creating Problems of Plenty. That such a large and unwieldy student body could not bode well for a school such as Wynberg-Allen that had prided itself in the motto 'Less is More' was amply evident in the poor school results in the Council Examinations for the year 1988.

Junior School staff resplendent in their centenary celebration attire, 1988.

The much-anticipated Centenary celebrations, however, were a cause for unadulterated joy all around. The hard work and planning of the past two years bore ample fruit. Nearly 3000 people were in attendance during the four-day gala from 6-9 June 1988. Lit up with thousands upon thousands of fairy lights, the School campus was decked out like a bride. Packed with entertainments and activities galore, the highlights included: Fancy Fair, school assembly, plays, slide shows, games, carnival, Founders' Day ceremony and a display of P.E. skills and gymnastics before the British High Commissioner, Mr and Mrs Fowler who were the Guests of Honour. A 900-seat Auditorium, the Kirby Laing Auditorium, also inaugurated on the occasion, soon became the pride and joy of the School and the setting for many a grave and joyous occasion till it was ravaged by a fire in 2009. Other building activities that were completed to coincide with the Centenary Celebrations were: a Junior School Swimming Pool, an extension

to the 110-seater Senior School Dining Hall as well as to the Dormitory above the Dining hall, an imposing gateway to the Senior School, among others.[5]

Shortly after the celebrations, on 1 August 1988, Mr Edwards handed over the baton to Mr K. P. Kuriakose, the Vice-Principal, who had joined as a physics master in 1985. In September 1988 Lt Col Skinner took over as Chairman from Rev Bowdish. While on the surface all seemed to be well, in reality something was terribly amiss. The majestic mountain ranges, the fresh crisp air, the luxuriantly forested campus teeming with animal life and resonant with bird-songs, in short, Nature in all its glory was present as ever before. However, what were also present were dark forces threatening to upset the School's hard-won equilibrium. Creeping up from the margins of human greed and pettiness, these dark powers were present both within and without: a certain section of the School staff had fallen prey to their insidious appeal and joined hands with larger forces massed outside the four walls of the School who were bent upon pursuing their own agendas. Decorum, decency and discipline — the three D's that had once been the hallmark of the School — had been slowly leaching out leaving the Spirit of Wynberg but a shadow of its former self. Steadily and inexorably the School was being pushed to the edge of a precipice. The shadows were lengthening and mischief-makers were enjoying a field day. Could this 100-year old institution check the momentum of its heedless push to its own doom? Could it pull back and save itself from toppling down into the abyss of nihilism? Could it redeem — in part if not whole — the pledge that men like Papa Biggs had made at the dawn of Independence when India had woken to freedom? ...Only Time could tell.

[5] To mark the Centenary Year, a history of the School was written by Ruskin Bond, Mussoorie's best-loved writer and also friend of Wynberg-Allen who stayed at Maplewood Cottage. The book is called *The Story of Wynberg Allen, Mussoorie.* A slim book, all of 40 pages, it nevertheless makes engrossing reading and is vintage Ruskin Bond.

1988 till present times

COURTESY: PAUL DEWARS

TURNING
THE TIDE
The Years of
Mellow Fruitfulness

To my God a heart of flame
To my fellow man a heart of love
To myself a heart of steel.

St. Augustine of Africa

Having crossed the 100-year mark, what the School needed at this crucial juncture of its history was stability, a time to consolidate its gains and not fritter away its immense goodwill in petty disputes and internal squabbles. Yet, stability was proving to be elusive with the School Principalship being marked by short-lived but tumultuous phases, unbridled interference from forces inimical to its smooth functioning and increasing interest in local

politics displayed by members of the staff. Mr K. P. Kuriakose's tenure as Principal, too, proved to be short, though in the time he had at his disposal he did attempt to give greater attention to outdoor activities as well as lay emphasis on co-curricular and extra-curricular ones. In the Annual Report for 1988-89, he noted:

> Our co-curricular programme is planned as an aid in learning and understanding those segments of the basic school curriculum that exist in the out-of-classroom situation. Further, it implements and makes enjoyable classroom teaching to a great extent, removes the fear of lack of knowledge from the mind of the learner by challenging him to extensive use of library and extra reading materials, and inspires students to keep going.

The Allen Auditorium before the fire, 1997.

The Duke of Edinburgh Award Scheme was introduced at Wynberg-Allen in 1989; it encouraged personal discovery and growth, self-reliance, perseverance, responsibility towards oneself and service to one's community.[1] It involved overnight hiking trips to Dhanaulti and Kanatal, cycling expeditions to the ONGC and the Forest Research Institute as well as conducting literacy and hygiene classes for the children of Class IV employees. Its activities were led by Mr Meston, Mr Nelson and Mr Kurian. In later years, the Literacy Club and the Village Project too would be taken under its wing.

[1] The Duke of Edinburgh Award Programme was first introduced in the United Kingdom in 1956. Its aim was to motivate young people aged between 14 and 25 years to become involved in a balanced programme of voluntary self-development activities to take them through the potentially difficult period between adolescence and adulthood.

And so things would have continued with the School scaling no new heights but also keeping itself safe from plunging into new depths, if it were not for the sudden resignation of Mr Kuriakose and the Headmaster Mr G. D. Rai on 27 May 1990. Once again, the School found itself in a state of uncertainty. The chaos and anarchy that had stalked the campus threatened to return, undoing the stability wrought by the six-year stint of Mr Edwards and unravelling the cloak of harmony that had been spun in the run-up to the Centenary celebrations. In an effort to instil confidence among staff and students and reassure them that they were neither rudderless nor cast adrift in turbulent waters, the Chairman, Lt Col Skinner moved into the school premises, and took over the day-to-day running of the school. Mrs R. A. Shah, the

The new Auditorium named after Sir Kirby Laing.

Mr T. W. Phillips with his wife Audrey.

much-loved Junior School Headmistress and among the senior-most faculty, rose to the occasion and filled in as the Senior School Headmistress.[2] But this was inevitably meant to be a short-term arrangement till a suitable person could be found and prevailed upon to take charge of the troubled School.

A highly suitable person was, indeed, found in Mr Terence W. Phillips who took over as Principal on 20 August 1990, ushering in an era of stability and all-round development. Having served as the Principal of La Martiniere College, Lucknow for four years, he brought with him a wealth of knowledge and experience — both as an educationist and administrator. His wife, Audrey Phillips, showed a natural talent for organisational details and was, therefore, appointed Assistant to the Principal and given charge of domestic affairs, welfare and counselling. At this time, the School had 1068 students on roll, with 292 boys and 139 girls in the Junior school and 140 day scholars; and 247 boys, 118 girls and 132 day scholars in the Senior school. Mr Phillips had inherited a large school, one with an illustrious legacy but also a recent history marred by confusion, chaos and controversies. In his first Principal's Report, Mr Phillips did not mince words when he acknowledged the challenges facing him:

> The task ahead of us at Wynberg-Allen is an uphill one. Much lies ahead of us to improve the academic standards, achievements in sports and other co-curricular activities and discipline, but above all the spiritual and moral fabric of the school. This is not an ordinary task but with our faith and trust in God, we can look forward with much hope for a brighter and more successful tomorrow.

[2] Mrs Roshanara Shah joined Wynberg in 1971. As a young widow with three small children (all of whom studied at Wynberg-Allen and went on to do extremely well for themselves in later years), she made the School her *karmabhoomi* during the 27 years of devoted service to this institution. Known to generations of old boys and girls for her mother-like love and care, she also proved to be a remarkably gifted administrator. Loved for her gentleness and non-controversial nature by staff and students alike, she now lives a retired life at 'Lawrence Terrace' (which she renamed 'Ashiana'), a short distance from the School. She was inducted into the Wynberg Homes Society in 1977, elected a member of the Board of Management in October 2002, and remains a popular figure on special occasions and prize days since her retirement in 1998.

In the first issue of the 'Alwynian' published at the beginning of his tenure, he once again admitted the gravity of the situation he had inherited; at the same time he expressed, in no uncertain terms, his expectations for the future:

> Wynberg-Allen has a heritage of faith that has upheld it in every crisis and the school community has always triumphed and grown in every

way through its trials. The School's infrastructure is as robust and resilient as ever, offering innumerable opportunities for physical, intellectual and spiritual development. Our blessings in 1991 have been manifold, and I have a vision that Wynberg-Allen has a future that we must all work unitedly for.

Urging the School community to gird their loins and move ahead with hope and faith, he initiated a series of reforms and also implemented several new ideas. The practice of an Open House for parents was initiated from 1991; its purpose was for parents to meet teachers and discuss their wards' performance in detail. The

Girls' dormitory.

academic year for 1992 began with a five-day workshop on 'team effectiveness' for the Senior school staff, followed by a similar one for the Junior school. Mr Phillips was adamant that the general academic standards needed to be improved at all costs, and he would brook no compromise in classroom teaching. Nor was any breach in discipline to be tolerated.

Mr T. W. Phillips with Siddhartha Basu on Founders' Day, 2005.

A slew of developmental projects were also initiated: a new dormitory for Class I and II girls with modern toilets and bathrooms; enhanced underground water storage capacity so that up to three days' water supply could be stored; renovations of the gymnasium; tapping of a new spring which was also linked to the main collection tank near the Wynberg stream thus vastly improving the water supply to the School; three new water pumps; building of staff quarters at Seven Oaks, among others. Within a year, the tattered fabric of school life had been considerably repaired, the rents caused by scandals and calumny darned up and the School's credibility as a Christian institution of repute and distinction restored. What is more, under Mr Phillips's leadership, it was decided that greater discretion needed to be shown in the School's admission policy and there was an urgent need to curtail the galloping enrolments for quality education to be imparted. In Mr Phillips's words:

> It is our constant endeavour to create among the staff and students a commitment to high ideals and standards, a deep-rooted urge for excellence in achievement in all spheres of school life and to instil in them the need for practical Christian living. With the liberal education that Wynberg-Allen has to offer and the emphasis on moral and spiritual values, character building and self-discipline, children who pass through its portals can claim to have had an all-round and balanced education which would help them face successfully the challenges of future life.

The School's concerns met with a positive response from the parents; they could see the change that was manifest in the School

life as also the overall improvement in ICSE results. To help deserving but needy students, the school set aside a considerable sum of money — to be used for grants and freeships. In the financial year 1993-94, 66 students were granted scholarships and a sum of Rs 4,90,000 was budgeted for this purpose. Financially, the School was now quite comfortably placed. Accordingly, the much-awaited and long-overdue revision in the salary scales and other benefits was brought into effect from 1 April 1994 for *all* categories of employees. This resulted in a far happier work force, one that was prepared to put behind the ill-will it had nurtured against the management through the turbulent 1980s and early 1990s. Henceforth, the School mantra was: Full Speed Ahead; both teaching and non-teaching staff put their weight behind the administration in a heightened display of solidarity and strength.

Regular maintenance of school buildings and staff quarters, enhanced facilities for single lady teachers and vastly improved mess and dining facilities created a feeling of prosperity and plenitude. Students' diet too became a subject of close scrutiny; the quality of food became comparable if not better than home-cooked, nutritious food and was provided in sufficiently large quantities. Parents were severely discouraged from sending unsuitable and unhealthy snacks. The

Tuck Shop began stocking healthy but tasty options so that the overall diet plan envisaged by the school authorities could be implemented.

Exposure to new ideas and new people — through workshops and interactions with visitors — motivated students to think differently and do things in better and more effective ways. Everywhere, there was evidence of the hand of God nudging the School along. Everywhere, there were signs of plenty. Finally, after many tortuous years of strife and discontent, the time to reap dividends had come. It was up to the

Top: Mrs Monica Lehmann. Above: Dr G. D. Lehmann, Chairman of the Board of Management.

School now: should it rest on its laurels or plough ahead? Should it sink back into the still waters of complacency or rise up to look for new horizons? Fortunately, it chose to do the latter.

Let not thy hand be slack.

Zeph 3.16

The tranquil tenor of School life was marred by tragic news from overseas. Monica Lehmann (nee Allen), the only surviving child of Henry Allen, passed away on 19 March 1994. What came as a cruel dual-blow was that close on the heels of this shock came the equally tragic news of her husband, Dr Lehmann's passing away on 15 April 1994. The Lehmann couple had been closely associated with the School for over 50 years and had always stood by the Wynberg-Allen community in good times and bad. A highly qualified medical doctor with a string of qualifications such as D. Phil., B. Sc. (Oxon), M.R.C.S., etc., Dr Lehmann (born 12 January 1904) had served the School Board as its Chairman for 37 years (from 1947-1984) creating a record of dedicated service to a cause dear to his heart. Quiet, gentle, self-effacing, Monica (born 25 May 1909) had a deep love for India; her husband, on the other hand, came from a German family with interests in the steel industry. Forsaking a lucrative career in metallurgy, he chose to specialise in eye surgery so that both he and Monica could serve the poor and needy among the hill-folk of Upper India, and set up the Herbertpore Eye Hospital. Their attachment to Wynberg-Allen kept pace with their professional commitments over the years, as they gave generously of their time and resources to both the Hospital and the School. When the time came for them to move on — incidentally within a few short weeks of each other — in keeping with their family's wishes, a Thanksgiving Service was held at the School in the memory of the Lehmanns on 16 April 1994. Their long years of association with the School and their unstinting efforts to raise money and build awareness for the work being done at Wynberg-Allen were remembered with gratitude and affection.

SCHOOL SONG

SHOUT "ALL HAIL" FOR WYNBERG-ALLEN,
SHOUT IT LOUD AND LONG;
OUR BELOVED ALMA MATER,
COME AND JOIN OUR SONG.

CHORUS

LIFT HER BANNER- ONWARD, UPWARD,
HEARTS AND VOICES HIGH;
SHOUT "EXCELSIOR", OUR MOTTO,
LET IT REACH THE SKY.

COME AND WEAR HER COLOURS GLORIOUS,
WEAR THE GREEN AND GOLD;
TO THE SCHOOL BE EVER LOYAL,
AND FOR TRUTH BE BOLD.

WHERESOE'ER HER CHILDREN STRUGGLE,
THEY RENOWN SHALL WIN;
INDIA'S FOES THEY'LL HELP TO VANQUISH,
AND TO CONQUER SIN.

EVER NOW FOR WYNBERG-ALLEN,
BACK THE SHADOWS ROLL;
AND GOD'S HOLY SPIRIT WATCHING,
GUIDE HER TO HER GOAL.

The political turmoil that had gripped much of Upper India from the early 1980s as demands for a separate state for the hill districts of Uttar Pradesh affected the small community at Wynberg-Allen too. The agitation to gain full statehood for Uttarakhand reached a bloody and violent crescendo when a mass movement erupted against the 27% reservation for Other Backward Castes (OBCs) in July 1994. By September, the situation had reached a boiling point with police firing on protestors in Khatima and Haldwani on 1 September and the next day, on 2 September, firing in Mussoorie killed seven people including the Deputy Superintendent of Police. Mass protests by people from all walks of life including students, women, etc. all over the hill districts brought life to a standstill. Things came to a head when on the night of 1-2 October 1994, the UP police fired on unarmed Uttarakhand activists — on their way to attend a rally in Delhi — at the Rampur Tiraha (crossing) in Muzaffarnagar district. Apprehensive parents rushed to take their children back home and the School perforce closed early with the academic year being severely dislocated due to protests and agitations.

Members, Wynberg Homes Society, 1993.

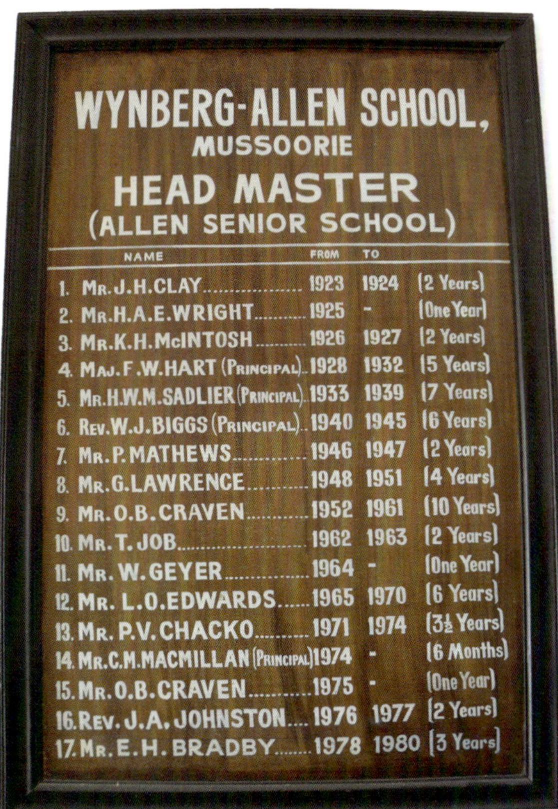

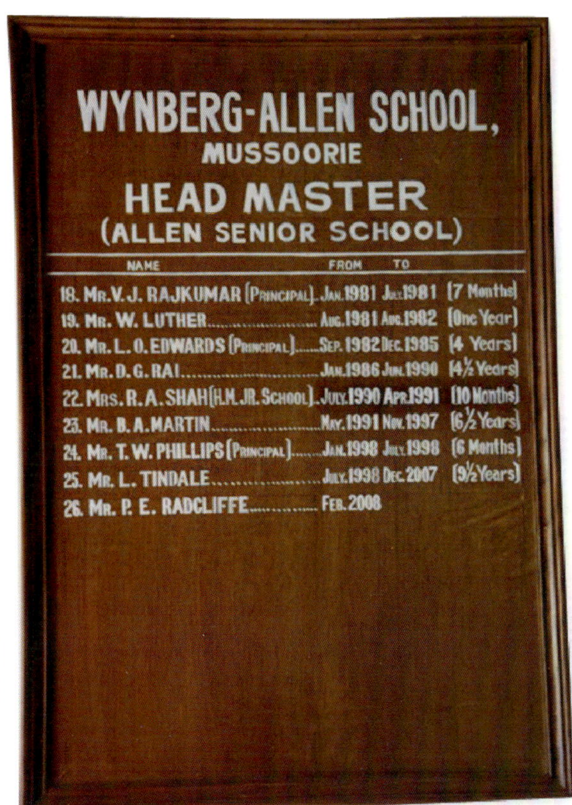

Despite the disruptions, the overall performance of the School remained good and examination results for 1995 proved to be gratifying. A handful of parents chose to withdraw their wards, preferring to send them to the plains far away from the turmoil in the hills; the great majority, however, chose to carry on in the belief that the School would do everything in its power to ensure the safety of the children under its care. Happily, the business of teaching and learning continued unhindered. So did the maintenance, renovation and development work: a gas-fuelled cooking range was installed in the kitchen, a brand-new generator took care of power breakdowns, toilets for Class IV employees were constructed, new colour television sets were bought for the boys' and girls' common rooms and the swimming pool was extended to 25 metres and enclosed with a fibreglass ceiling.

As the School developed quietly and surely, it gained valuable experience from every opportunity that came its way. On 22 April 1995, a team from the Maidenhead Hockey Club visited the School, bringing with them a whiff of internationalism and palpable excitement. Two former students, Lionel Connor and Bertie Kettle, accompanied the team. A hockey match was played with the visiting team followed by tea causing much merriment and exchange of views.[3] Then, on 23 November 1996, a special guest came for the Prize Day: this was David Sadleir, former Australian Ambassador to China and, more importantly for the School, son of the former Principal H. W. M. Sadleir.

The ICSE and ISC (Class XII) results that had been displaying a steady improvement showed a spectacular flowering in March 1996 with Poornima Aggarwal securing an aggregate of 94.6% in five subjects. Career guidance and counselling were introduced from the following year to help students choose the right vocation. Also, the unwieldy and large student body was trimmed over a period of time to a more manageable size. By September 1997, the school reported 731 students on its rolls; the School hoped to further reduce numbers by ruthlessly sending away more admission-seekers than ever before and exercising greater discretion in who they chose to admit by scrutinising the parents' profile more carefully than ever before. Soon, word spread about the 'exclusivity' of Wynberg-Allen which no doubt helped the School maintain its rigorous standards of discipline and protocol.

In keeping with the Christian spirit that had guided it from its infancy and the Christian faith that still formed the bedrock of

Facing page: Heated swimming pool, Senior School.

[3] Upon his return to the UK, Lionel Connor narrated with great enthusiasm all that he had seen and heard. In particular, the singing of the hymn 'Abide with Me' by the School choir moved him. The School ties brought back by the Old Boys, were treated like gold dust and worn with great pride at School reunions and, sadly, the funerals that happened with alarming frequency. Incidentally, a perusal of the Old Boys' Newsletters shows how much the alumni enjoy visiting their old school assured as they are of a warm welcome whenever they return. The School remains an important site for them also because – years after they have left – of the enduring bonds of friendship they had forged decades ago, ties that have endured across continents and survived historical and political events and crises.

WYNBERG ALLEN
1888

WYNBERG-ALLEN-MUSSOORIE-1888-
EXCELSIOR

its existence, the School strove to do all it could for needy Christian children. For the year 1997-98 it gave scholarships to 56 students from a budgeted amount of Rs. 1,171,325. In addition, it also disbursed scholarships from the dividends it received from Dunsterville Allen plc of England in which the School had been donated 47,991 Ordinary Shares valued at 20 p each, the dividend from which had been set aside for a Christian Workers' Childrens' Fund from the previous year. The money received from the annual Fancy Fair was also diverted towards a fund for needy children called the Wynberg-Allen Scholarship Fund. Gone were the days when the small amounts collected during Fancy Fair went a long way in buying much-needed essentials and meeting costs.

The unexpected passing away of Brigadier Skinner on 17 March 1999 in Epsom, UK brought grief to the School community that had benefitted greatly from his wisdom and guidance during its period of strife and uncertainty. For, it was Brigadier Skinner who had steered the School towards calm waters and helped ensure a period of stability. His association with the School over a period of two decades, first as Vice-Chairman and later as Chairman and officiating Principal till the arrival of Mr Phillips, had helped in no small measure in bringing the School to its present eminence. Having served in the battlefields of Persia and Italy during the

Second World War and in the North West Frontier Province and having been a career soldier with the elite Cavalry Regiment Skinner's Horse — the regiment founded by his illustrious great-great-grandfather James Skinner — he knew well enough that victory required great teamwork though defeat could often result from the poor judgement of one individual. The funeral service held at the School in his honour on 29 March 1999 quoted from the following observation made by Mary Lee Hall:

> If I should die and leave you here awhile
> Be not like others sore, undone
> Who keep long vigils by the silent dust and weep,
> For my sake turn again to life and smile
> Nerving thy heart and trembling hands to do
> Something to comfort other hearts than thine
> Complete these dear unfinished tasks of mine
> And I perchance may therein comfort you.

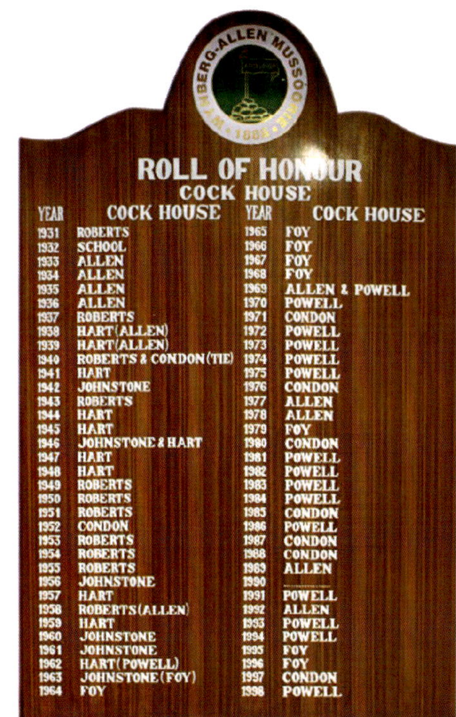

Brigadier Skinner's successor, Mr S. C. Singha who had hitherto been associated with the School as Vice-Chairman of the Board of Management, proved to be most suited to devote himself to those 'dear unfinished tasks'. A retired IAS officer, he brought a renewed sense of selfless devotion to a cause, a characteristic that had marked the men and women who had been associated with the School during its early years. Mr Singha's long and distinguished career, which had begun with teaching at St Edwards' College in Peshawar, had included stints in Burma during World War II as well as Escort Officer to Lord Mountbatten during the Transfer of Power years, and long years in various administrative posts in the U.P. Hills Division.

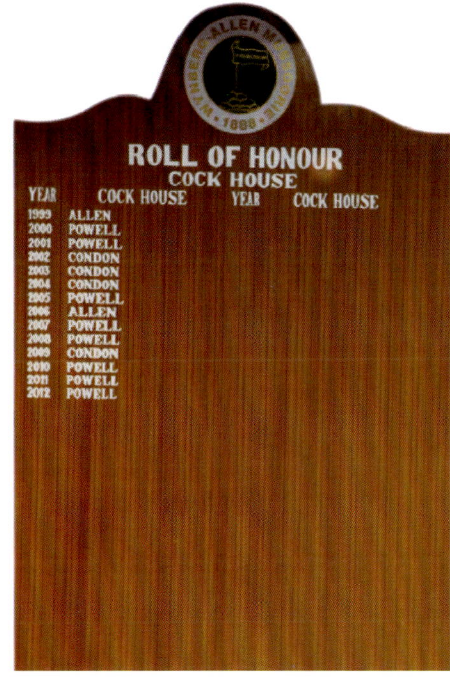

A steady stream of distinguished visitors exposed the staff and students to new ideas and new ways of seeing things: John Hardless, an alumnus, presided over the Junior School athletics on 4 October 1997 and marvelled at the sea change the school had undergone since his own schooldays. Another Old Boy, Carl

A. Phillips, accompanied by his wife Maureen, were the Guests of Honour at the Senior School athletics on 10 October 1997. Impressed by the good work he saw being done, Carl Phillips pledged a sum of Rs. 52,000, invested with the Steel Authority of India, and used for an annual award for 'Innovation' in any area of school life. The following year, Dr Anil Wilson, Principal of St. Stephens College, Delhi, arrived as the Guest of Honour on the 110th Founders' Day on 4 June 1998. The year 1999 was especially hectic in terms of overseas visitors. Dr Fred Burke, Director, Overseas Examinations, University of Cambridge, gave a presentation on new testing patterns for examinations. Inez Gibbons, Senior Education Advisor, Canadian Education Centre,

spoke on educational opportunities in Canada. Dr Jurgen Chopard of the International Centre in Gilon, Switzerland, delivered an audio-video presentation on careers in hotel management and tourism. A three-day career guidance and counselling programme was conducted for 130 students from Classes X-XII by counsellors from the Institute of Career Studies, Lucknow. Bishop Stanley Downes, retired Bishop of the Methodist Church of India who had graduated from Allen in 1944, delivered the Founders' Day Address on 3 June 1999. The Bishop reminded his young listeners of all the little things that comprised his many happy memories, namely: receiving four annas for 'tuck' in the weekly letter from his father; learning to swim in a brewery tank called Whymper's

ROLL OF HONOUR
SCHOOL CAPTAINS

YEAR	BOYS' CAPTAIN	GIRLS' CAPTAIN
1964		H. BELLEW
1965	J. S. BHATIA	J. BROWNE
1966	S. MARWAH	S. KAUR
1967	CHAMPA NAMGYAL	S. PAWA
1968	N. PAWA	S. BROWNE
1969	P. SINTHOKIOW	S. CHOWDHURI
1970	M. BHUTIA	A. SINGH
1971	V. SACHDEV	S. ROY
1972	R. KAPOOR	C. HOUGHTON
1973	P. N. AMIN	SONAM LHADRON
1974		
1975	J. KHANDPUR	
1976	G. SACHDEV	
1977	P. CHAUDHARY	H. KAURA
1978	S. GYATSO	ANITA BOSE
1979	S. GATSO	
1980		GRACE THOMAS
1981	N. DARUKA	RIGZIN DOLKAR
1982	VIPUL KISHORE	RENUKA GRUNDY
1983	KULBIR SINGH	H. NARULA
1984	RAGHUBANSH SINHA	CHHABI AGGARWAL
1985	HEMANT BISHT	CHHABI AGGARWAL
1986	LALREMRUATA	NANHI SINGH
1987	SYED M. HUSSAINI	TSERING W. DHOMPA
1988	AAKASH BANSAL	VANDANA V. SINGH
1989	ABHAY SINGH	HELENA RAJ
1990		SHALINI KHULLAR
1991	VINIT SINGH	RUHI MAHAJAN
1992	HIRDAY PAL SINGH	ANGELINE D. MALAGAR
1993	RAJAN NARULA	RUNJHUN AGARWAL
1994	BENJAMIN LIANZAMA	POOJA JAISWAL
1995	ANAND PRAKASH	UMA TANDON
1996	MANDHIR SINGH SAHNI	
1997	AMIT JAISWAL	NITI CHAUDHARY
1998	AVINASH AGARWAL	RACHNEE THURAKIJIKAN

ROLL OF HONOUR
SCHOOL CAPTAINS

YEAR	BOYS' CAPTAIN	GIRLS' CAPTAIN
1999	DEEPAK BHATIA	POOJA CORNELIUS
2000		TENZIN TSOMO
2001	AZIZ SHRESTHA	GARGI GOGIA
2002	KUNWARJIT SINGH	RUCHNAN NARULA
2003	MOHIT VERMA	AKIRA DHAKWA
2004	BIRAJ BABU MALLA	
2005		ISHITA DUTTA
2006	AMANDEEP SINGH CHABRA	PARINEETA JANE DAS
2007	ADITYA JAIN	
2008	SHERAF SONAM	SURBHI GLORIA SINGH
2009	GURJEET SINGH GILL	PRACHI SINGH
2010	VISHAL MODI	SAKSHI GUPTA
2011	MOHIT RUPANI	PRAKRITI KATARIA
2012	KIRTIVARDHAN SINGH	T. SEDONLA UKYAB LAMA

Pool some distance down the hill from Allen; being part of the AFI Guard of Honour for the visiting Viceroy and fainting in the hot sun; acting in school plays like 'Charley's Aunt' and 'The Monkey's Paw'; getting beaten by Saeed Jaffrey for the first place in the Scripture Class; hanging out at the Lookout Rock near the Science Lab; trooping up to Union Church twice every Saturday and catching a sight of the girls coming down from the Landour side making the trek somewhat less arduous!

With the brand new state of Uttarakhand finally coming into existence from 9 November 2000, Dehradun became the new

state capital and Mussoorie, home to many of the state's oldest and finest schools, emerged as a new centre of learning. The myth of hill schools being quaint, old-fashioned places of seclusion was busted as the limelight once again shone on their achievements. The vernacular and mainstream press lavished attention on their activities and recorded their achievements for the benefit of a larger, appreciative public. The seat of provincial power was no longer in distant Lucknow; it was now but a stone's throw away. State-level bureaucrats and technocrats began to take a renewed interest in the shabby but gracefully ageing 'Queen of the Hills'. The community at Wynberg-Allen, too, basked in this new-found attention. At the same time, it kept itself abreast with developments on the national front. As the proxy war with Pakistan waged on the icy heights of Kargil and the death toll of Indian casualties mounted, the School collected funds to the tune of Rs. one lakh in 1999 and sent it to the Army Central Welfare Fund for the families of soldiers killed or disabled during the Kargil Operation.

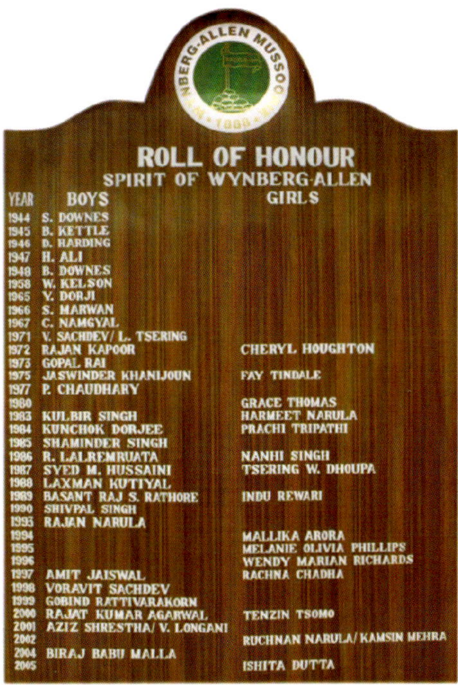

Ever now for Wynberg-Allen,
Back the shadows roll;
And God's Holy Spirit watching,
Guide her to her goal.

School Song: 'Excelsior'

Standing at the threshold of the new millennium the School felt itself — justifiably one might well add — equipped to deal with the challenges that the New Age might throw its way. At the dawn of the year 2000, taking stock of its gains and losses, hits and misses, strengths and balances it found the scales tipping in its favour. Its student strength stood at a healthy 646. The games programme — always a compulsory component of school life — continued to fetch laurels. Examination results showed a healthy upswing year after year. What is more, the school now

WYNBERG-ALLEN-MUSSOORIE
1888
EXCELSIOR

had more money in its kitty than ever before. A healthy portfolio of investments meant an assured income over and above that generated through fees or interest accrued on capital funds. In the ten years of Mr Phillips's stewardship, the School had not only regained its lost poise but also equipped itself to meet the demands of a new age. Academically, spiritually, morally, financially, it found itself on a surer footing than ever before. In the field of Information Technology, spearheaded by Leslie Tindale, the School could boast of having taken greater strides than most other schools in the vicinity. Hooper Hall had been fitted with state-of-the art audio-visual equipment and the use of multimedia as a teaching aid made teaching both fun and vastly more accessible. Computerised Report Cards were implemented and two well-equipped Computer Labs introduced IT to every facet of School life.

With the passing of Mr S. C. Singha on 9 May 2003, Dr David G. Fiol took over the Chairmanship. Dr Fiol who had earlier served on the Board of Management made the following astute observation:

> So I read the report [for the year 2004] and looked for something which I could elaborate on — something perhaps unusual, spectacular; or, conversely, something that showed a significant problem area. As I read and discovered nothing in either category I realised that such long-term consistency in excellence is itself unusual and even spectacular. Many advertisements for the mushrooming numbers of schools these days proclaim their vision for all-round excellence and holistic education. But one looks at the total programme of Wynberg-Allen and the special qualities of our students passing out into life and realises that we already have a school which has long put such visions into dynamic action. It has become a way of life here. So we all have come to **expect** this as the norm. This attitude of ours is most unusual and takes us pleasantly by surprise.

The year 2004 saw yet another feather in the School cap when Mr Phillips received the National Award for Teachers (Principals

Mr Phillips receiving an award from the President.

category) at a glittering award ceremony at Vigyan Bhawan. This well-deserved honour was bestowed by no less a person than the President of India, Dr A. P. J. Abdul Kalam. The Award, an annual feature, is conferred by the Department of Secondary and Higher Education, Ministry of Human Resource Development, Government of India.

However, since all things must come to an end and change is the only constant in life, Mr Phillips's tenure as Principal came to an end in 2006; and with it ended a long and glorious chapter in the annals of the school, for here was a highly competent academician who institutionalised change and development to take the School into the 21st century. His 16 years at the helm were the second longest innings as Principal (second to Rev Biggs who had served for 18 years in the same capacity); it was also, by far, the most productive in terms of growth and development. He was succeeded

by Mr Albert Temple who took over from 1 July 2006 but could not continue beyond 14 months. Evidently, this was a time of tremendous responsibility — both for those who were giving away the responsibility and those taking charge. Since the School could not be left headless, the Board requested Mr Phillips to return from his well-earned retirement in Pune and pitch in till a suitable and permanent solution could be found. For the Phillipses it was a case of 'Once more into the breach, my friends, once more!' as they came back to fill in their old positions from June-December 2007.

A worthy successor was eventually found — literally in the bosom of the Wynberg-Allen family — in Leslie Tindale, an Old Boy of the batch of 1981 who had joined the school in 1991 to teach Computer Science and was serving as Headmaster since 15 July 1998. He took over as Principal on 1 January 2008. In the words of the Chairperson (incidentally the first woman to serve the

Mr Leslie Tindale.

School in this capacity), Mrs F. Keelor,[4] Mr Tindale is a 'product of the School, by the School, and for the School'! Much liked by staff and students for his genial disposition and calm good sense, Leslie Tindale took to the job like the proverbial duck to water. Having known the school intimately (for not only had he and his siblings studied here so too had his mother and aunt as well as his father and a host of cousins), he knew better than most its strengths and weaknesses. Fully aware as he was of the School's past,

[4] Mrs Florence (Flo) Keelor, chairperson of the Board from 2005 to 2010, was Principal of La Martinere Girls' College, Lucknow between 1978 and 1997. Mr Jonathan (John) Mason, briefly succeed her as Chairman between 2010 and 2011. He taught in various schools and was Headmaster of Doon School from 1996 to 2003 after which he returned to the Varkey Group to manage several of their schools in the UAE before his retirement. Both were seasoned and highly capable educational stalwarts. They brought with them the benefits of their vast experience and helped steer the School towards stronger academic and overall development. While both voluntarily relinquished their post as chairperson, they continue to serve on the Board of the School.

he knew how to steer this 120-year old institution into modern times without losing any of its core values and ethos.

Under Mr Tindale's leadership, the School continued to grow and evolve. It also learnt to cope with minor hiccups and losses, the most tragic being the loss of the Sir Kirby Laing Auditorium that was destroyed in a fire on the night of 28-29 March 2009. On the fateful night, the School was alerted by the staff of the Jaypee Residency Manor Hotel in Barlowgunj as well as the St George's College who spotted the first flames from across the valley and

immediately sent help. Soon, help poured in from the townsfolk in Mussoorie as well as civic agencies from Dehradun. While the fire was stopped from spreading to the rest of the campus with the timely and ingenious use of water from the swimming pool when the Fire Engines ran dry, the Auditorium was reduced to nothing more than a mangled heap. Noting this loss in the Annual Report, Mr Tindale observed:

> True to the spirit of the School, out of adversity came new resolve and thanks to the positive attitude and initiative of the entire Wynberg-Allen family, school life continued as normal with every activity being held on schedule and with as much success as before.

The Auditorium was rebuilt within a year; if anything it was better designed and equipped than before. It was dedicated by Bishop Stanley Downes on 3 June 2011 in the presence of Mr Terence Phillips in his capacity as Vice-Chairman of the Board of Management. Further developmental work was undertaken by adding four more apartments to the existing two-storied staff quarters at Seven Oaks, an Activity Centre, two multi-purpose outdoor courts and health centre. Once again, voicing the deep-seated sense of satisfaction that prevailed on the School campus, Mr Tindale concluded his Annual Report with the following words:

> ... it is the deep feeling of conviction that the well-being, success and happiness of the Wynberg-Allen family is a living testimony to the character and growth of our school.

The Dalai Lama came visiting again, after a gap of nearly 50 years, on 17 September 2012. He was welcomed by the Principal, Mr Leslie Tindale with the following words:

> Adding to the immense honour bestowed upon Wynberg-Allen by his presence is the generosity of His Holiness in agreeing to visit,

> for the second time, at extremely short notice and despite a packed schedule. It is truly with bated breath that we wait to hear His Holiness and to have the opportunity to interact with and learn from him.

The Dalai Lama expressed his delight in coming to Wynberg-Allen once again for, no matter what his schedule and time constraints, the opportunity to be with young people and to be able to interact with them was always a prime incentive for him; what is more, the School's contribution towards the education of Tibetan children was a subject dear to his heart:

> Time is always moving on and no force can stop it. My own generation, people over 60 or 70 belong to the twentieth century, which is now over and gone. People like these who are less than 20 years old truly belong to the twenty-first century. They will shape the future.

When asked what surprised him most about humanity, His Holiness answered:

> Man. Because he sacrifices his health in order to make money. Then he sacrifices money to recuperate his health. And then he is so anxious about the future that he does not enjoy the present; the result being that he does not live in the present or the future; he lives as if he is never going to die, and then dies having never really lived.

Tragically, Mr Phillips passed away on 23 March 2013 while this book was in the process of being written. He had taken over as Chairman of the Board in 2011 and was fully engaged in the administration of the School. Whilst he was looking forward to a jubilant Quasquicentenary celebration, his vision was for Wynberg-Allen to carve for itself a place amongst the premier educational institutions in India. His fervour and his firmness of purpose will linger among all who knew and loved him. In the words of an old student, 'As a person Mr Phillips was most caring,

Facing page: His Holiness the Dalai Lama with Mr Leslie Tindale and Mr Terence Phillips.

compassionate and gentle; as a professional he was unwavering in his beliefs and commitment.'

As the School gears up to celebrate 125 years of its existence with a slew of gala events in the year 2013, Mr Tindale sums up his School's present status thus:

> The school continues to build on its foundation of Protestant Christian principles and looks to equip our students to face the world as we know it today. At the speed at which change intensifies and technology mushrooms and explodes at a breathtaking pace,

fresh challenges emerge each day. As our founders wished, at Wynberg-Allen School our aim is still unchanged — to provide every one of our students with self-respect, dignity and the space and opportunity to grow into citizens of our country, fully prepared to use technology and new advancements in science and the corporate world but always and ever remaining grounded in the deep and unshakeable traditions and heritage bequeathed to us. We believe that our boys and girls, utilising the variegated opportunities available to all the students of the school, will grow into young gentlemen and ladies who are embodiments of the school motto 'Excelsior', always striving to reach yet higher and go one step further. Finally, as at the beginning, the entire gamut of excellence in academic work, sports, co-curricular activities and character and personality development is enclosed within the great orb of service to others — both at school and to the wider community.

Present-day Wynberg with the newly-laid Basketball Court.

Afterword

Looking back, it has indeed been such a long journey! From one ramshackle rented bungalow on a deserted hilltop to a sprawling campus spread over 130.5 acres. From a lone intrepid woman who doubled up as Superintendent and teacher to a teaching faculty of 50, and a non-teaching staff of 30. From precisely two children on its rolls (both orphans) to a student strength of 730 in 2013. From a few hundred rupees scraped together with the kindness and generosity of well-meaning friends and philanthropists to a significantly substantial corpus. From a fee of Rs. 15 to an average fee of Rs. 1.5 lakh per year per boarder child. While the numbers speak for themselves and despite this phenomenal leap in every sphere of School life, the educational purpose at Wynberg-Allen has remained constant. The School's aim was, and continues to be, to provide a sound education in a healthy environment. The vision of its founders was, to quote Mr Tindale: 'to train young people for responsible citizenship in an epoch that was witnessing bewildering change and unparalleled challenges. The school pledged to send forth a steady stream of such young men and women to enrich the nation and serve the world. To accomplish this great mission, our founders noted that this could only take place if the students were imbued with a sense of dedication to God, devotion to duty and a desire to serve, regardless of their vocation.'

The tiny seed that was planted in Jaberkhet one hundred and twenty-five years ago has indeed grown to be a strong and magnificent tree with its roots going deep into the soil, its branches sturdy and solid, its foliage dense and lush. The men and women associated with the School from its earliest days were remarkable for their vision and commitment. Evidently, those who chose the School Motto did well to take their inspiration from the poem by H. W. Longfellow for it encapsulates the never-say-die spirit of its founders who thought of nothing except moving on, from strength to strength:

A youth, who bore 'mid snow and ice

A banner with the strange device, Excelsior.

The School's motto, Excelsior, was inspired by a poem by H. W. Longfellow.

Clearly, it is 'the banner with the strange device' that continues to spur the community at Wynberg-Allen to move ever higher, onward and upward.

R. J.

Bibliography

PRIMARY SOURCES
Documents:

Minutes of Board of Management Meetings

Principal's Reports

Auditor's Reports

School Magazines

Alumni Newsletters

Interviews:

Terence and Audrey Phillips

Leslie Tindale

Michael Sen

Reverend G. Cornelius

Paul Cornelius

R. A. Shah

Cynthia Burrell

Hugh and Colleen Gantzer

Ganesh Saili

Bill Aitken

Pramode Sawhney

A. B. Misra

Champa Dhakpa

SECONDARY SOURCES
Documents:

The Himalayan Gazette, Different Volumes, Lal Bahadur Shastri Academy, Mussoorie.

The Dehradun Gazette, Different Volumes, Lal Bahadur Shastri Academy, Mussoorie.

Articles/Books:

Aitken, Bill. 2003. *Footloose in the Himalayas*. Delhi: Permanent Black.

Anthony, Frank. 2007. *Britain's Betrayal in India: The Story of the Anglo Indian Community*. Second Edition. London: The Simon Wallenberg Press.

Atkinson, E. T. 1981. *The Himalayan Gazetteer. Vol III, Part II.* (reprint). New Delhi: Cosmo Publications.

Banerjee, Juliet. 2012. *The Gap-Toothed Banister: A Tale of Anglo-India*. New Delhi: Niyogi Books.

Bond, Ruskin. 1988. *The Story of Wynberg Allen, Mussoorie*. Mussoorie: Art Printing Press.

Caplan, Lionel. 2001. *Children of Colonialism: Anglo-Indians in a Postcolonial World*, Oxford: Berg.

Caplan, Lionel. 2003. *Colonial and Post-Colonial Hybridities: Eurasians in India.* IIAS Newsletter, No. 30, March. Shimla: Institute of Advanced Studies.

D'Souza, Austin, A. 1976. *Anglo-Indian Education: A Study of its Origins and Growth in Bengal up to 1960*. Delhi: Oxford University Press.

Fisher, Michael H. 2007. 'Excluding and Including "Natives of India": Early-Nineteenth-Century British-Indian Race Relations in Britain', *Comparative Studies of South Asia, Africa and the Middle East* 27 (2): 303–314 [304–5].

Gaikwad, V. R. 1933. *The Anglo-Indians: A Study in the Problems and Processes Involved in Emotional and Cultural Integration*. New York: Asia Publishing House.

Hawes, Christopher J. 1996. *Poor Relations: The Making of a Eurasian Community in British India*, 1773-1833. London: Curzon.

Jones, Edith, M., Caroline Wilkie and Mary I. Mcgee. 1954. *Woodstock School: The First Century, 1854-1954*. Mhow: Rasalpura Vocational School.

Kennedy, Dane. 1996. *The Magic Mountains: Hill Stations and the British Raj*. Berkley: University of California Press.

Mitra, Chandan. 1987. *Constant Glory: La Martiniere Saga, 1836-1986*. New Delhi: Oxford University Press.

Monk, Mauger Fitzhugh (1828-1849). 2012. *Letters of a Mussoorie Merchant*. Introduced by Ruskin Bond and edited by Ganesh Saili. New Delhi: Niyogi Books.

Nabar, Vrinda and Nilofer E. Bharucha (eds.). 1994. *Postcolonial Perspectives on the Raj and its Literature*, Bombay: University of Bombay.

Roy, Arindyo. 2006. *Civility, Literature and Culture in British India, 1822-1922*. New Delhi: Routledge.

Saili, Ganesh. 2010. *Mussoorie Medley: Tales of Yesteryear*. New Delhi: Niyogi Books.

Saili, Ganesh. 2012. *Gupp and Gossip from the Hills*. New Delhi: Niyogi Books.

Stoler, Ann Laura. 1989. 'Rethinking Colonial Categories: European Communities and the Boundaries of Rule', *Comparative Studies in Society and History*, 31: 134-161.

'The Rambler' (of 'The Mussoorie Times'), 1936. *A Mussoorie Miscellany*. Mussoorie: Mafasalite Press.

Williams, Blair. R. *Anglo-Indians: Vanishing Remnants of a Bygone Era.*

Wright, Dean, R. and Susan W. Wright. 1971. 'The Anglo-Indian Community in Contemporary India.' *Midwest Quarterly* XII, Winter, pp. 175-185.